趣味識字
Fun with Chinese
A Chinese Character Learning Curriculum

第七冊

Workbook 7

自序

我是一位在美國的自學媽媽，孩子的中文學習完全由我親自教導。

在傳統教學方式的薰陶下許多家長認為孩子學中文必須先從注音開始，往往也認為中文字筆畫眾多複雜對小孩來說太難。其實對幼兒來說每一個中文字都只是一個圖案，幼兒的記憶力非常強，認字對他們來說並不困難。

我自己的兩個孩子都是從認字開始學習中文的。當初我會設計趣味識字是因為在市面上並沒有找到令我完全滿意的教材，絕大多數的教材都是從注音符號或是筆畫簡單的字開始教學。雖然筆劃較少容易書寫但往往這些字在日常生活上並不常見，在孩子的世界裡更是沒有應用的機會。而市面上認字的教材卻普遍地缺乏動手的參與感。孩子在學習的過程中常常覺得教材枯燥乏味，既沒趣味又缺乏實用性。這樣的學習對孩子來說不但痛苦也沒有效率。使用這些教材後我發現自己一直在動手製作輔助教材來提昇孩子的學習興趣。

我一直深信一定要讓孩子覺得有趣和實用，他們才會有學習的動力，有了動力才會學得好。所以趣味識字的設計是以先教常用字的方式讓孩子能夠快速進入閱讀，因而發覺識字的實用性。當孩子懂得如何應用文字後，學習自信自然就提高了。製作輔助教材時為了幫助孩子加強對生字的記憶，除了使用字卡和遊戲的方式複習，我也設計了一系列的遊戲習題，而這些習題就是趣味識字誕生的前奏。

最後非常感謝您選擇趣味識字做為孩子的教材，也希望這套教材可以幫助您的孩子快樂學習中文。

Preface

I am a homeschooling mom in America who successfully taught my two children to read Chinese at a young age.

Many people think that learning Chinese must start with pinyin because Chinese characters are too complicated and believed to be too difficult for children. However, in children's minds, each Chinese character is just like a picture and memorization is not difficult for them.

Both my children learned to read Chinese beginning with character recognition, yet the process was not easy for me. Existing textbooks often start teaching with pinyin or start with rarely used characters with minimal strokes for writing. Books that emphasize character recognition also tend to be less interactive and less hands-on causing the learning process to be tedious and unmotivating for children. I found myself constantly needing to create my own teaching materials while using these textbooks; and this is the reason for the creation of Fun with Chinese.

Fun with Chinese is designed to teach the most commonly used Chinese characters first, quickly allowing children to be able to read meaningful phrases and sentences from the very beginning. Pictures and games are also used to help with character retention, and each lesson includes reading passages to review previously learned characters.

Today, I am sharing with you this wonderful system that I have used with my own children and hoping to make your child's Chinese learning an easy and enjoyable journey.

— Anchia Tai

關於英文翻譯

習題本中的句子都有中英雙語,希望讓中文不是很好的家長們也有辦法使用教材。其中朗讀句子練習中的英文翻譯也盡量讓句型和中文相對應幫助英文為母語的家長容易理解。

About the English Translations

The English translations in the workbooks are specifically designed in a way to closely match up with the Chinese sentence grammar structure. While this might make the translations grammatically incorrect in English, the design will help English speakers to learn and understand the Chinese sentences better.

關於筆順

本書中的國字筆順是依據中華民國教育部「常用國字標準字體筆順學習網」的筆劃順序彙編。中華民國教育部對於部分筆順有做調整,可能於傳統書寫筆順有所差異,不同華人地區的筆順也可能有所不同。如果本書中的筆順與家長所學的筆順有所差異,請自行調整教學。

About the Stroke Orders

The stroke orders of the characters in this workbook follow the stroke orders provided on the "Learning Program for Stroke Order of Frequently Used Chinese Characters" website of the Ministry of Education, R.O.C. (Taiwan). The authors are aware that there were changes to the stroke orders made by the Ministry of Education as well as regional differences in character stroke orders. Please feel free to make adjustments in teaching if the stroke orders are different in your region.

每當完成一課後請回到本頁將該課的愛心塗上顏色。
Please color a heart after you have completed a lesson.

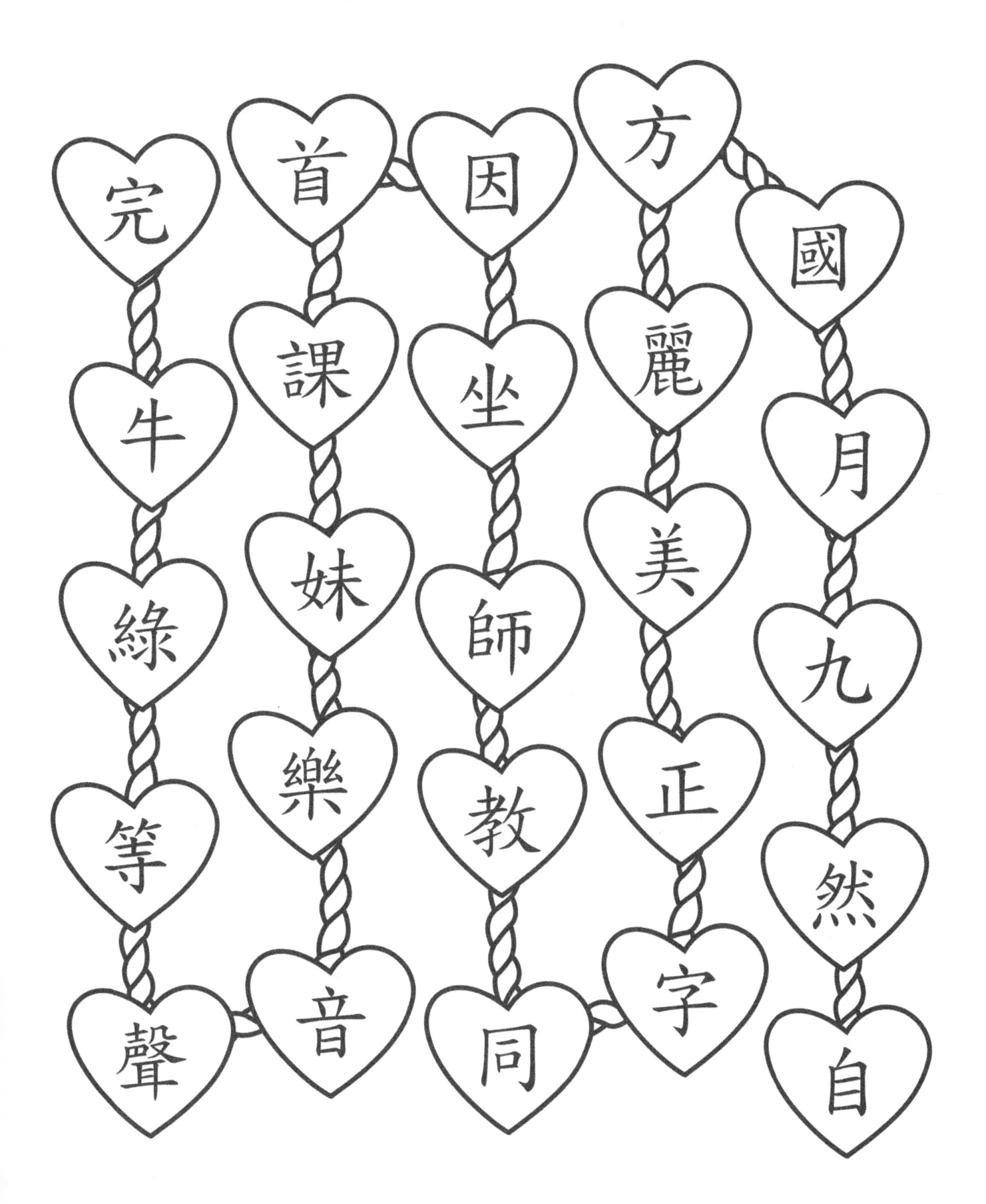

1

完	首	因	方	
牛	課	坐	麗	國
綠	妹	師	美	月
等	樂	教	正	九
聲	音	同	字	然
				自

第一課

Lesson 1 Wán – finish; whole

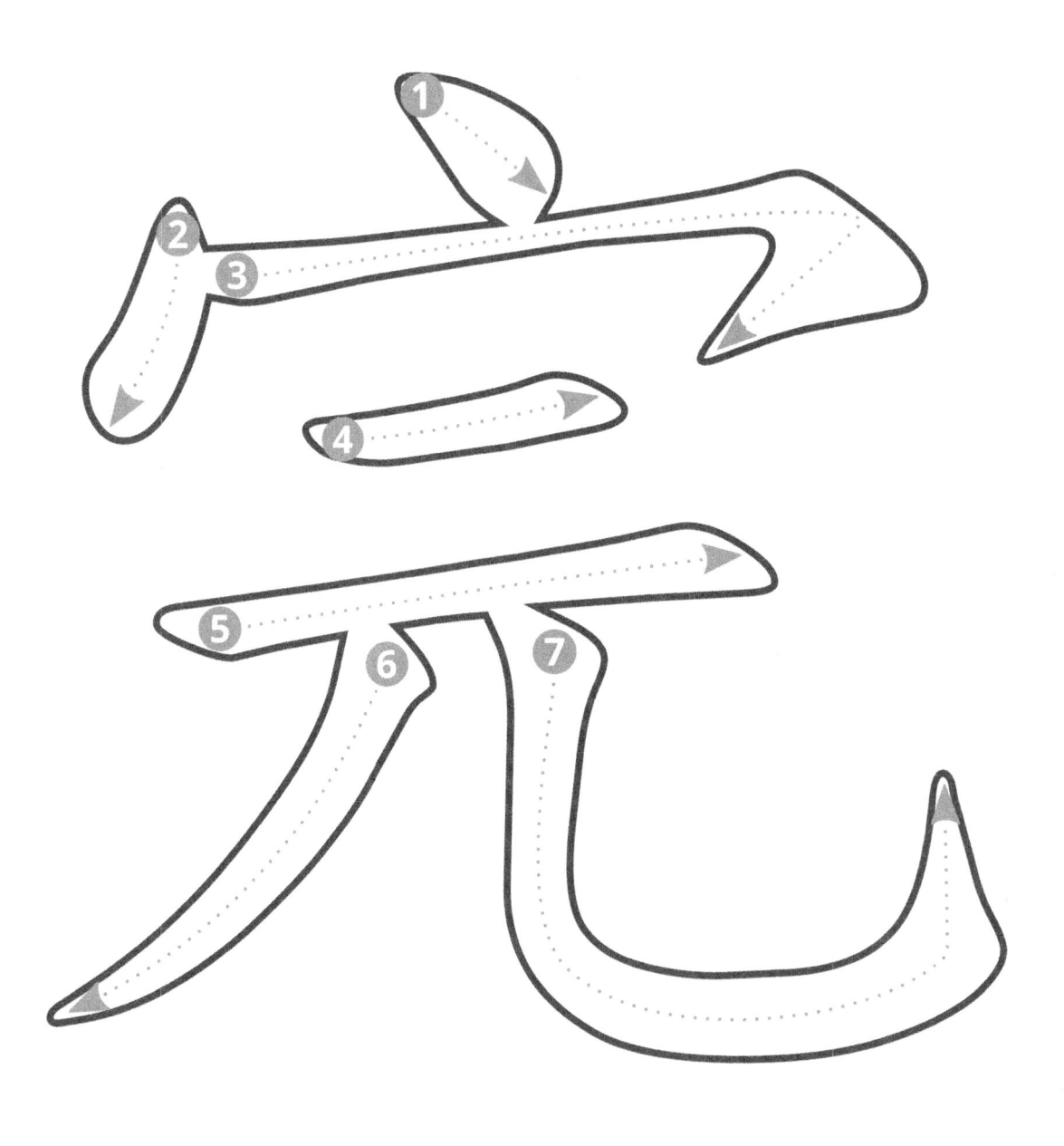

本書中的國字筆順是依據中華民國教育部「常用國字標準字體筆順學習網」的筆劃順序彙編。
The stroke orders of the characters in this workbook follow the stroke orders provided on the "Learning Program for Stroke Order of Frequently Used Chinese Characters" website of the Ministry of Education, R.O.C. (Taiwan).

跟著「完」字從 ➡ 到 ★ 走出迷宮。
Follow the characters 完 from the arrow to the star to exit the maze.

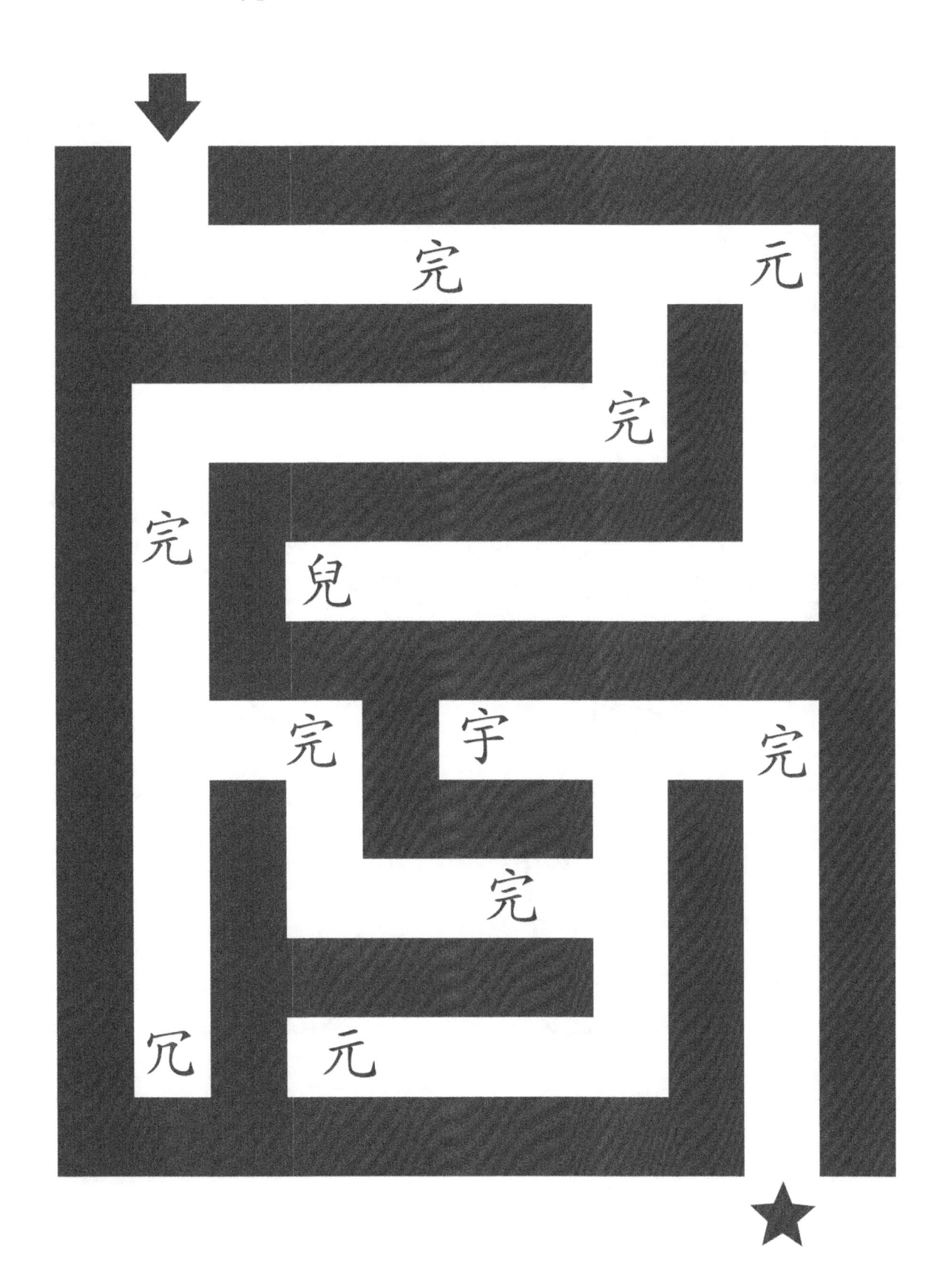

4

請將有「完」字區域塗上黑色。
Please color the areas with the character 完 black.

唸唸看
Read-Aloud

- 媽媽說先看完書再出去玩。
  Mom says to first finish reading then go out to play.

- 可是先看完書，天就已經黑了。
  But if (I) finish reading first, it will already be dark.

- 還是先玩完再看書好。
  It is still better to finish playing first then read.

- 媽媽說：「不對，先看書好。」
  Mom says, "No, it is better to read first."

- 你說媽媽對還是我對？
  Is Mom correct or am I correct, what do you say?

恭喜你完成了這一課，請回到第一頁將本課的愛心塗上顏色。
Congratulations! You have completed a lesson. Please color the heart for this lesson on page 1.

第二課

Lesson 2 Niú – ox; cow

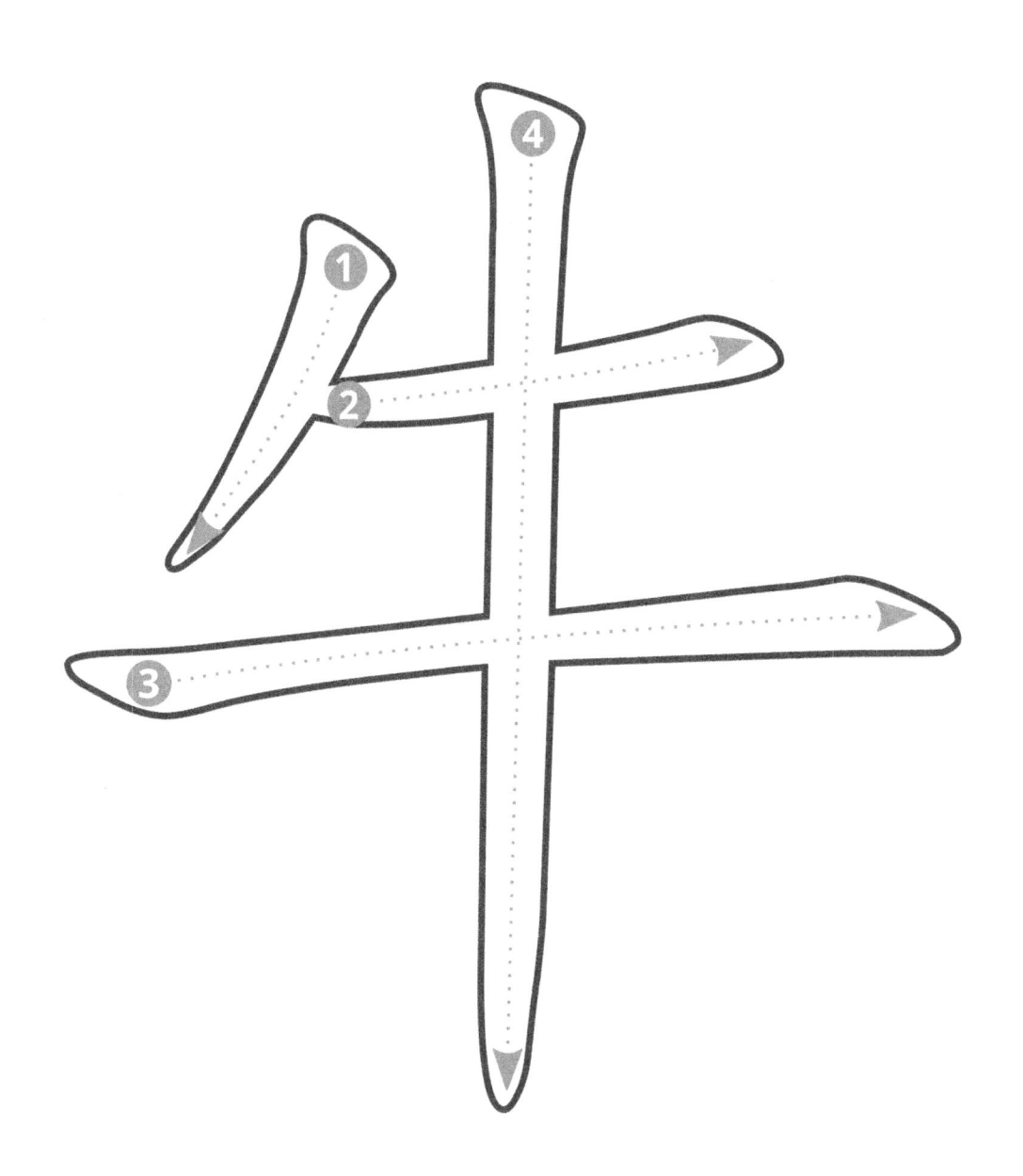

本書中的國字筆順是依據中華民國教育部「常用國字標準字體筆順學習網」的筆劃順序彙編。
The stroke orders of the characters in this workbook follow the stroke orders provided on the "Learning Program for Stroke Order of Frequently Used Chinese Characters" website of the Ministry of Education, R.O.C. (Taiwan).

「牛」是象形字，它是由牛頭的樣子演變而來的。
The character 牛 is a pictograph. It looks like a bull's head.

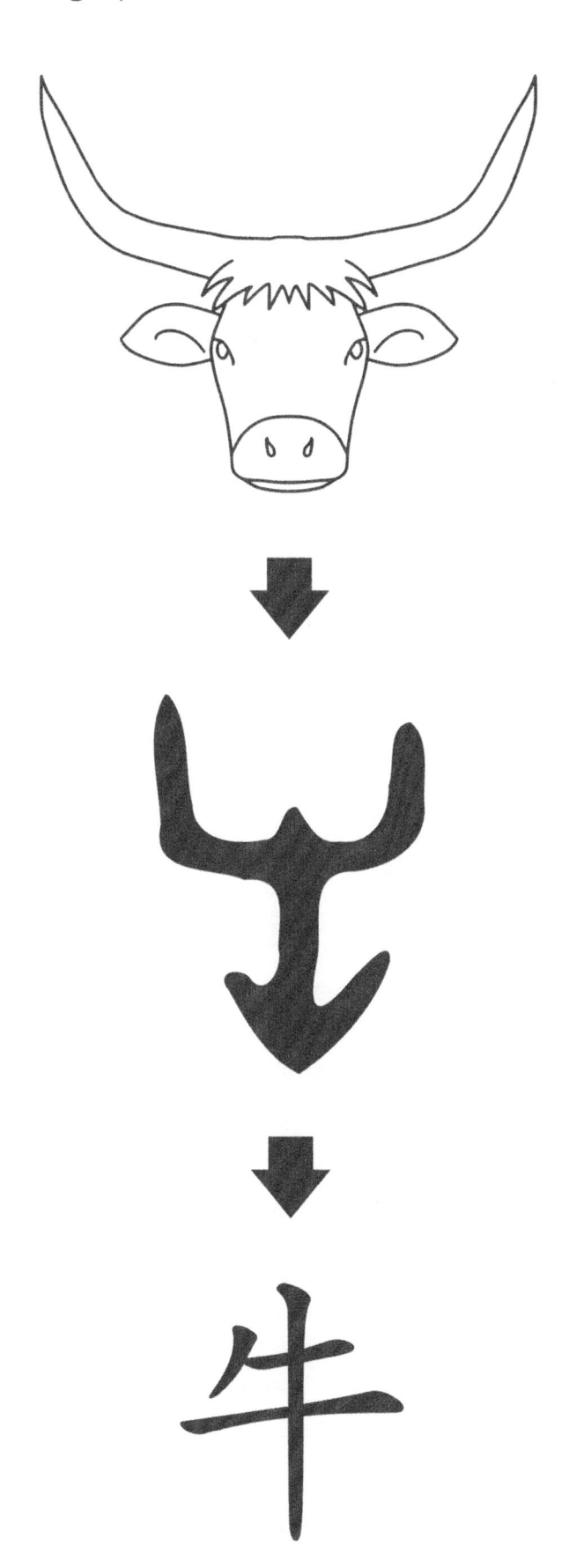

8

連連看
Connect the characters to the correct pictures.

牛 ●

狗 ●

貓 ●

連連看

唸唸看
Read-Aloud

- 我想要寫一本故事書。
  I want to write a story book.

- 裡面要有一隻黑色的貓和一頭黃色的牛。
  In the story, there will be a black cat and a yellow cow.

- 貓和牛常常一起出去玩。
  The cat and the cow often go out to play together.

- 寫完後我會先給你看。
  After I finish writing, I will show it to you first.

- 寫完這本以後我還要再寫一本。
  After I finish writing this book, I will write another one.

恭喜你完成了這一課,請回到第一頁將本課的愛心塗上顏色。
Congratulations! You have completed a lesson. Please color the heart for this lesson on page 1.

10

第三課

Lesson 3 Lǜ – green

本書中的國字筆順是依據中華民國教育部「常用國字標準字體筆順學習網」的筆劃順序彙編。
The stroke orders of the characters in this workbook follow the stroke orders provided on the "Learning Program for Stroke Order of Frequently Used Chinese Characters" website of the Ministry of Education, R.O.C. (Taiwan).

請將青蛙塗成綠色並唸出下方的文字。
Please color the frog green and read aloud the characters below.

我是綠色的

12

請將三個相同的字連成一線。
Please connect the same characters to win the tic-tac-toe.

紅	紅	綠
藍	紅	綠
藍	藍	綠

唸唸看
Read-Aloud

- 綠綠的草地上有一頭老牛。
On the green grass, there is an old cow.

- 他工作完了所以在吃草。
It finished working, therefore, it is eating grass.

- 他先吃綠色的草再吃黃色的草。
It first eats the green grass then eats the yellow grass.

- 老牛吃了好多好多草。
The old cow ate a lot of grass.

- 草都沒了。
There are no more grass.

恭喜你完成了這一課,請回到第一頁將本課的愛心塗上顏色。
Congratulations! You have completed a lesson. Please color the heart for this lesson on page 1.

第四課

Lesson 4 Děng – to wait; rank; class

本書中的國字筆順是依據中華民國教育部「常用國字標準字體筆順學習網」的筆劃順序彙編。
The stroke orders of the characters in this workbook follow the stroke orders provided on the "Learning Program for Stroke Order of Frequently Used Chinese Characters" website of the Ministry of Education, R.O.C. (Taiwan).

找出到達「等」字的路。
Find the path leading to the character 等.

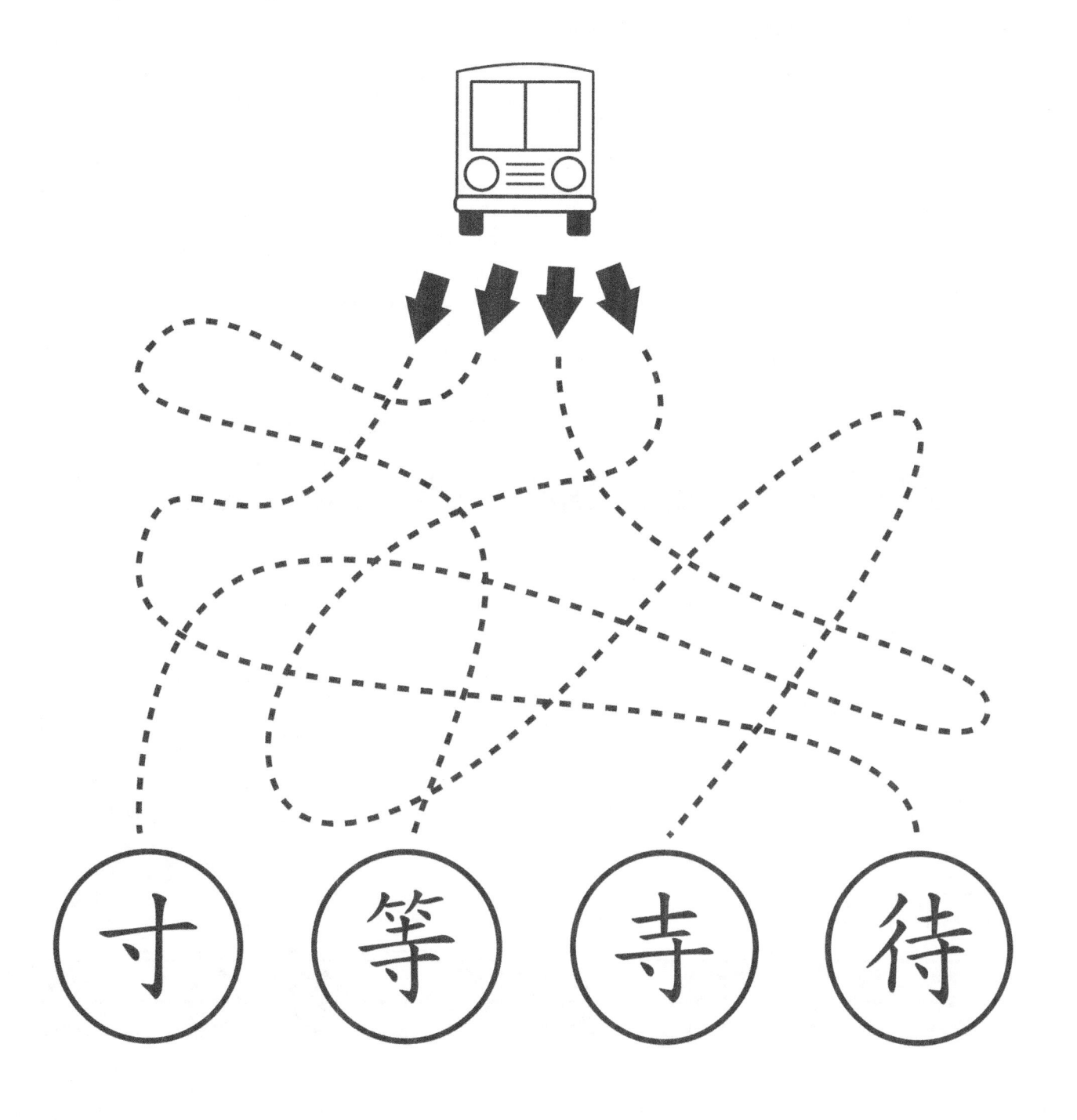

寸　等　寺　待

16

請剪下下方的字格貼到正確的車箱中並唸出車箱上的文字。
Please cut out the characters at the bottom, paste them into the correct cargo, and read aloud the characters on the trains.

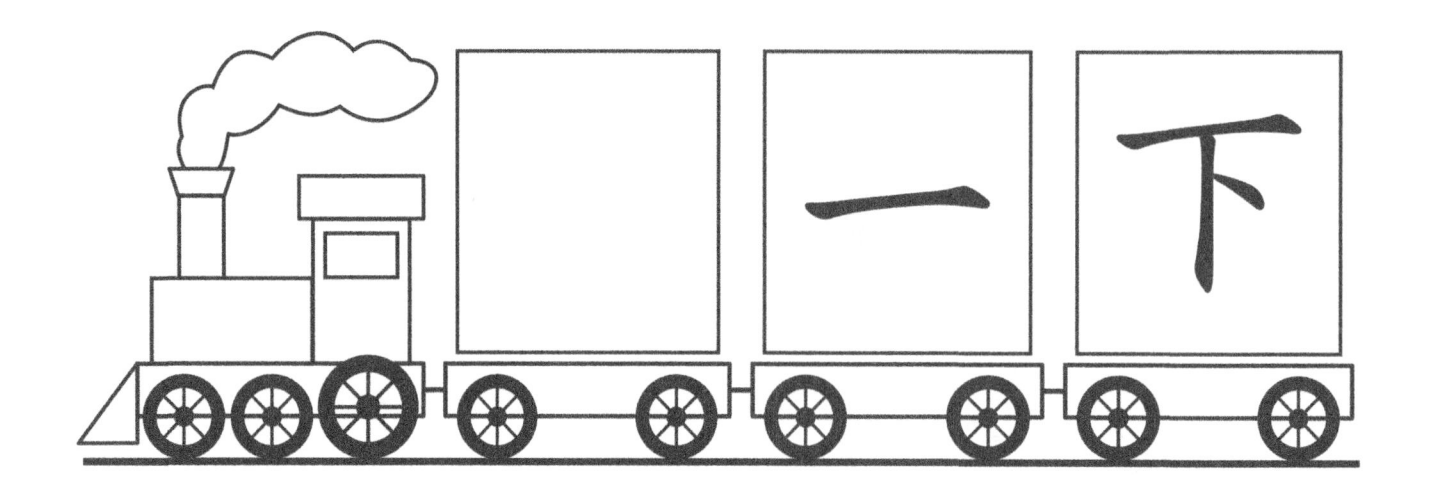

一 下

我

等 寸 等 寺 等

唸唸看
Read-Aloud

- 等一下小牛和小鳥要去山上玩。
Later the little cow and the little bird are going up the mountain to play.

- 高山上有白白的雲和綠綠的樹。
On the high mountain, there are white clouds and green trees.

- 小鳥先飛到山上等小牛。
The little bird flies to the mountain first to wait for the little cow.

- 去完山上又去小鳥家。
After going to the mountain, (they) went to the little bird's home.

- 玩了一天真開心。
(They are) so happy from playing whole day.

恭喜你完成了這一課，請回到第一頁將本課的愛心塗上顏色。
Congratulations! You have completed a lesson. Please color the heart for this lesson on page 1.

第五課

Lesson 5 Shēng – sound

本書中的國字筆順是依據中華民國教育部「常用國字標準字體筆順學習網」的筆劃順序彙編。
The stroke orders of the characters in this workbook follow the stroke orders provided on the "Learning Program for Stroke Order of Frequently Used Chinese Characters" website of the Ministry of Education, R.O.C. (Taiwan).

請剪下字格並將「大聲」貼在可以大聲說話的時候,將「小聲」貼到應該安靜的時候。

Please cut out the phrases at the bottom and paste 大聲 next to situations when you can be loud and 小聲 next to situations when you should be quiet.

大聲　小聲　大聲　小聲　大聲

將「聲」字塗色，幫瓢蟲找到樹葉。
Color the characters 聲 to find the path to the leaf.

唸唸看
Read-Aloud

- 小鳥在綠色的樹上等小牛。
  The little bird is waiting for the little cow on the green tree.

- 他一邊等一邊歌唱。
  It sings while waiting.

- 他的歌聲很好聽。
  Its voice is very soothing.

- 他的歌聲大家都愛聽。
  Everyone loves to listen to its singing.

- 唱完了小牛也到了。
  When it finishes singing, the little cow arrives.

恭喜你完成了這一課,請回到第一頁將本課的愛心塗上顏色。
Congratulations! You have completed a lesson. Please color the heart for this lesson on page 1.

第六課
Lesson 6 Yīn – sound; noise

本書中的國字筆順是依據中華民國教育部「常用國字標準字體筆順學習網」的筆劃順序彙編。
The stroke orders of the characters in this workbook follow the stroke orders provided on the "Learning Program for Stroke Order of Frequently Used Chinese Characters" website of the Ministry of Education, R.O.C. (Taiwan).

將有「音」字的音符著色。
Color the musical notes with the character 音.

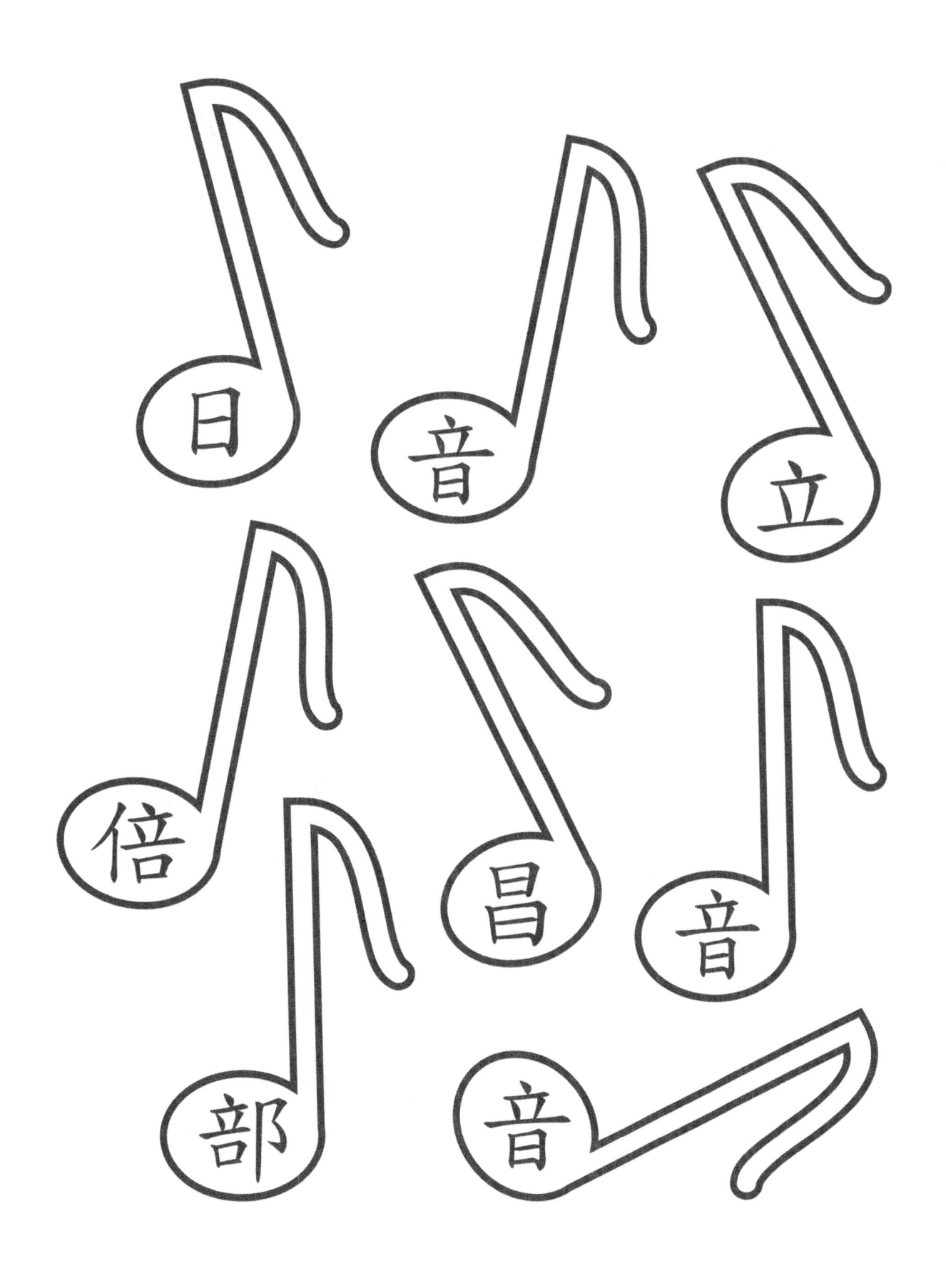

24

請將「音」字連到會發出聲音的物品。
Connect the character 音 to the objects that make sounds.

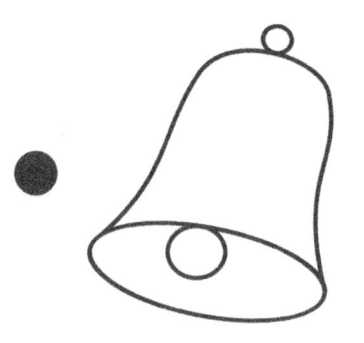

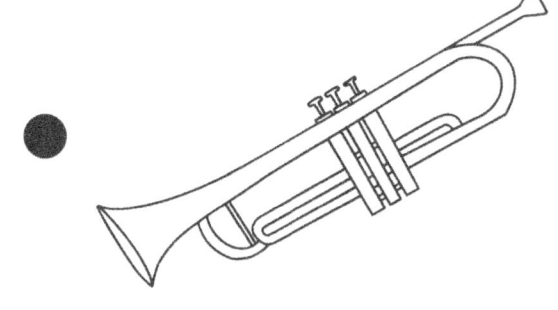

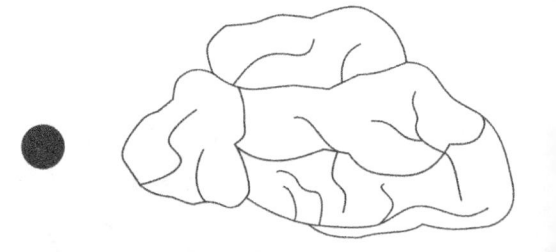

音

唸唸看
Read-Aloud

- 我和小牛在綠草地上。
The little cow and I are on the green grass.

- 小牛問：「那是什麼聲音？」
The little cow asks, "What is that sound?"

- 我說：「那是爸爸說話的聲音。」
I say, "That is the sound of Dad talking."

- 小牛又問：「我們幾點回家？」
The little cow asks again, "What time are we going home?"

- 我說：「七點就回家。」
I say, "(We will) go home at seven o'clock."

恭喜你完成了這一課，請回到第一頁將本課的愛心塗上顏色。
Congratulations! You have completed a lesson. Please color the heart for this lesson on page 1.

26

第七課

Lesson 7 Lè – happy
Yuè – music

本書中的國字筆順是依據中華民國教育部「常用國字標準字體筆順學習網」的筆劃順序彙編。
The stroke orders of the characters in this workbook follow the stroke orders provided on the "Learning Program for Stroke Order of Frequently Used Chinese Characters" website of the Ministry of Education, R.O.C. (Taiwan).

請圈出所有快樂的表情並唸出下方的文字。
Please circle all the happy faces and read aloud the characters below.

我們很快樂

28

請將「音樂」一詞連到與音樂有關的東西。
Connect the phrase to the objects that are related to music.

音樂

唸唸看
Read-Aloud

- 弟弟在綠草地上聽音樂。
  (My) little brother is listening to music on the green grass.

- 他聽著聽著就唱起來了。
  He starts to sing while listening.

- 他唱歌的聲音很好聽。
  His singing voice is very pleasant.

- 他唱歌唱得很快樂。
  He sings happily.

- 等一下他就會回家。
  Later he will go home.

恭喜你完成了這一課,請回到第一頁將本課的愛心塗上顏色。
Congratulations! You have completed a lesson. Please color the heart for this lesson on page 1.

第八課

Lesson 8 Mèi – younger sister

本書中的國字筆順是依據中華民國教育部「常用國字標準字體筆順學習網」的筆劃順序彙編。
The stroke orders of the characters in this workbook follow the stroke orders provided on the "Learning Program for Stroke Order of Frequently Used Chinese Characters" website of the Ministry of Education, R.O.C. (Taiwan).

連連看
Connect the characters to the correct family members.

爸爸　　　媽媽　　　妹妹

請圈出正確的答案。
Please circle the correct answers.

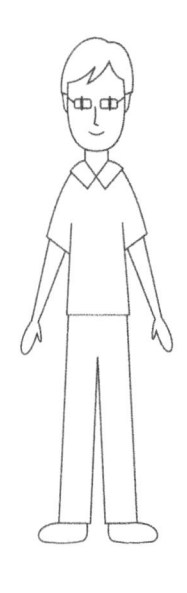

妹妹／爸爸

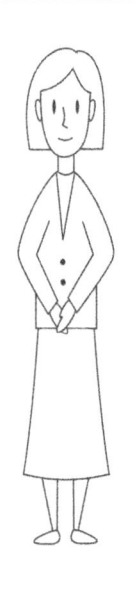

媽媽／弟弟

奶奶／妹妹

唸唸看
Read-Aloud

- 弟弟和妹妹都愛聽音樂。
  (My) little brother and (my) little sister both love listening to music.

- 妹妹的聲音很好聽。
  (My) little sister's voice is very pleasant.

- 我要和弟弟妹妹一起去學唱歌。
  I will learn to sing with (my) little brother and (my) little sister.

- 他們沒有等我就走了。
  They left without waiting for me.

- 所以我生氣了。
  Therefore, I am upset.

恭喜你完成了這一課,請回到第一頁將本課的愛心塗上顏色。
Congratulations! You have completed a lesson. Please color the heart for this lesson on page 1.

第九課

Lesson 9 Kè – class; lesson

本書中的國字筆順是依據中華民國教育部「常用國字標準字體筆順學習網」的筆劃順序彙編。
The stroke orders of the characters in this workbook follow the stroke orders provided on the "Learning Program for Stroke Order of Frequently Used Chinese Characters" website of the Ministry of Education, R.O.C. (Taiwan).

請將下方的字格剪下來讓孩子選擇正確的語詞貼上。
Please cut out the phrases at the bottom and paste the correct ones.

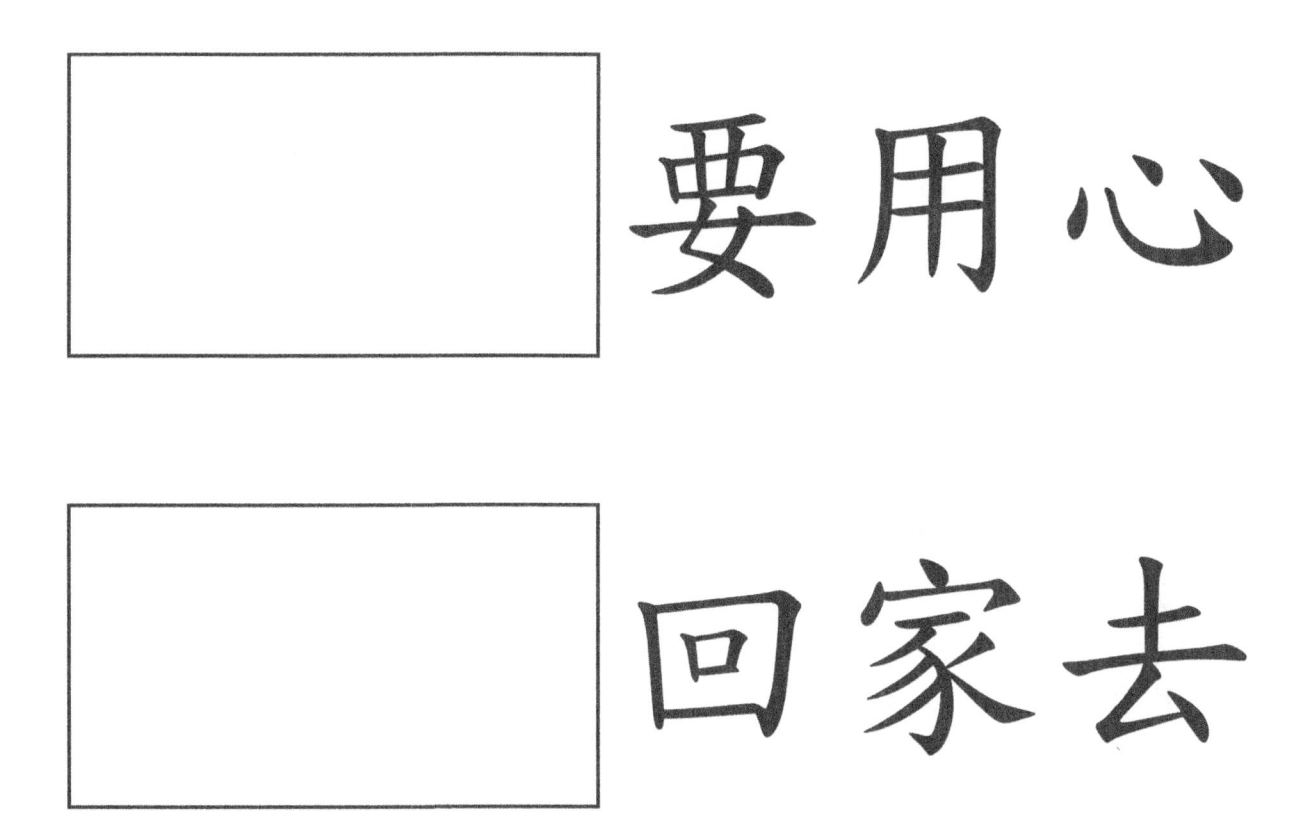

☐ 要用心

☐ 回家去

| 上課 | 下課 |

36

請將上課會用到的東西連到正確的課程。
Please connect the objects to the correct lessons.

中文課

音樂課

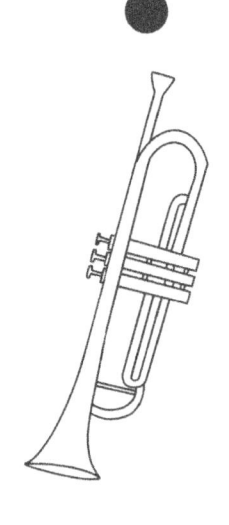

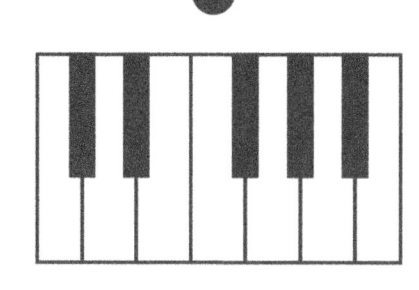

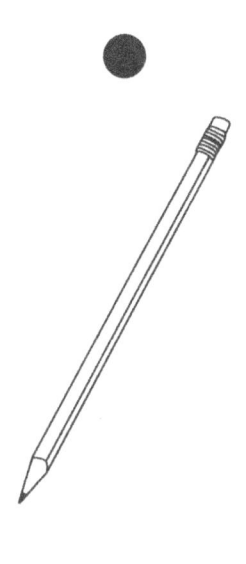

唸唸看
Read-Aloud

- 妹妹去上音樂課。
  (My) little sister went to music class.

- 他的歌聲很動聽。
  Her singing voice is very touching.

- 妹妹下課後一路唱著歌回家。
  After class, (my) little sister sang all the way home.

- 回家後又唱了三小時。
  After (she) got home, (she) sang for another three hours.

- 我也一起唱了兩小時。
  I also sang for two hours together (with her).

恭喜你完成了這一課，請回到第一頁將本課的愛心塗上顏色。

Congratulations! You have completed a lesson. Please color the heart for this lesson on page 1.

第十課

Lesson 10 Shǒu – head; first; classifier for poems, songs etc.

本書中的國字筆順是依據中華民國教育部「常用國字標準字體筆順學習網」的筆劃順序彙編。
The stroke orders of the characters in this workbook follow the stroke orders provided on the "Learning Program for Stroke Order of Frequently Used Chinese Characters" website of the Ministry of Education, R.O.C. (Taiwan).

跟著「首」字從 ➡ 到 ★ 走出迷宮。
Follow the characters 首 from the arrow to the star to exit the maze.

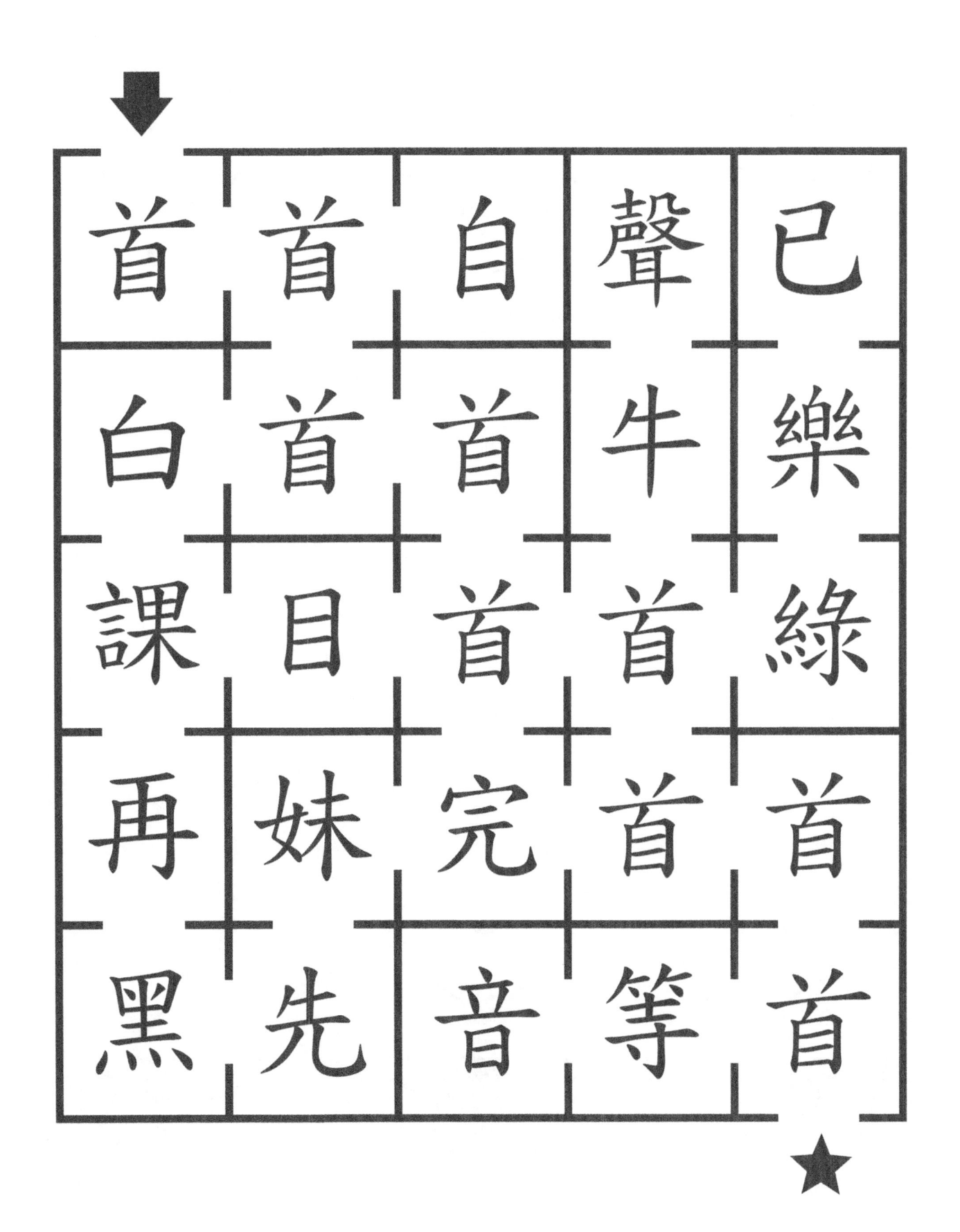

首	首	自	聲	已
白	首	首	牛	樂
課	目	首	首	綠
再	妹	完	首	首
黑	先	音	等	首

40

連連看一樣的字。
Draw lines to connect the matching characters.

課　　妹　　首

首　　妹　　課

連連看一樣的字。

唸唸看
Read-Aloud

- 妹妹在音樂課上學了四首歌。
  (My) little sister learned four songs from music class.

- 有一首歌叫《小白花》。
  There is one song called Edelweiss.

- 他從來都不唱給我聽。
  She never sings (it) for me.

- 你聽過這首歌嗎？
  Have you heard this song before?

恭喜你完成了這一課，請回到第一頁將本課的愛心塗上顏色。
Congratulations! You have completed a lesson. Please color the heart for this lesson on page 1.

第十一課

Lesson 11 Yīn – cause; reason; because

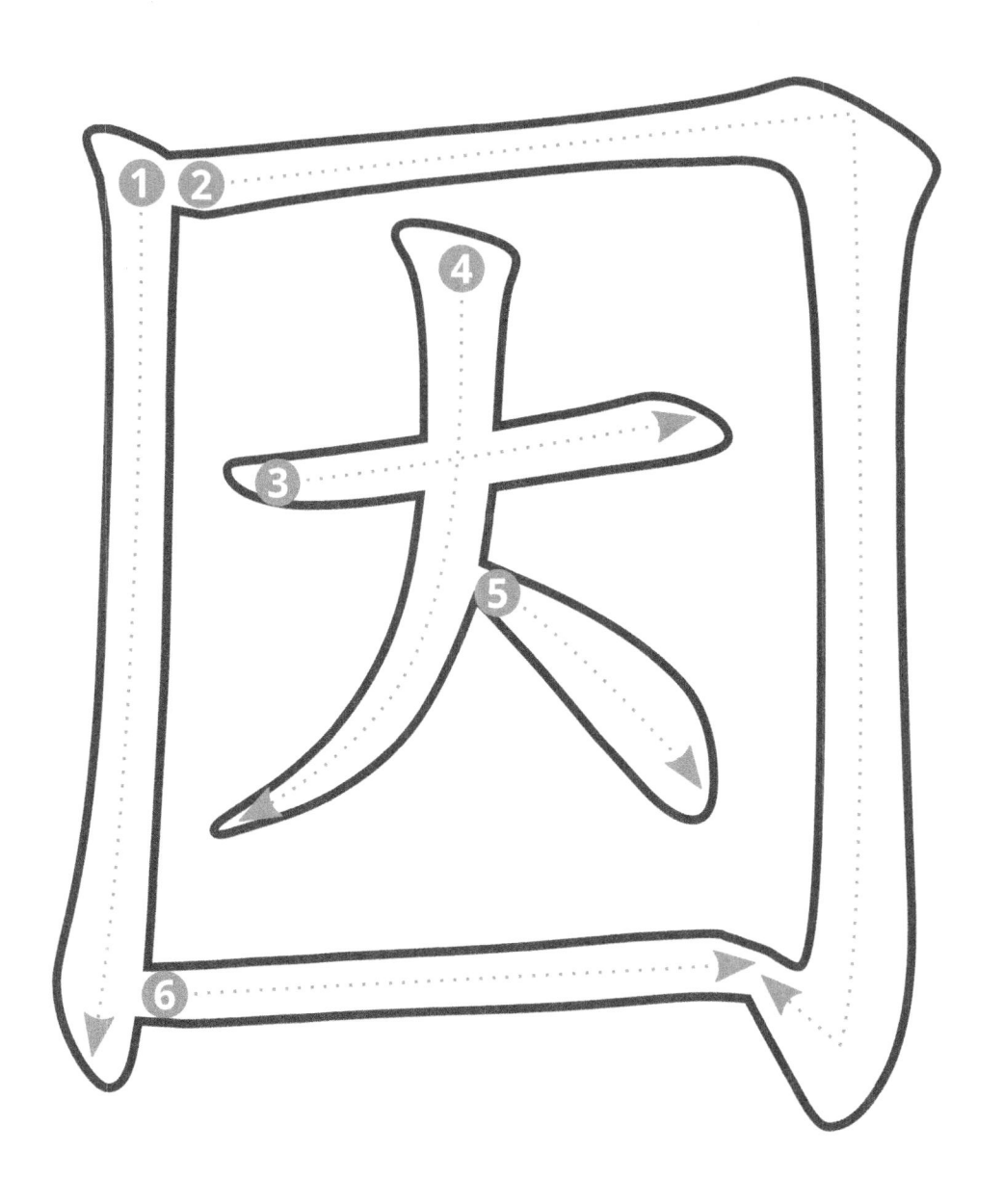

本書中的國字筆順是依據中華民國教育部「常用國字標準字體筆順學習網」的筆劃順序彙編。
The stroke orders of the characters in this workbook follow the stroke orders provided on the "Learning Program for Stroke Order of Frequently Used Chinese Characters" website of the Ministry of Education, R.O.C. (Taiwan).

跟著「因」字從 ➡ 到 ★ 走出迷宮。
Follow the characters 因 from the arrow to the star to exit the maze.

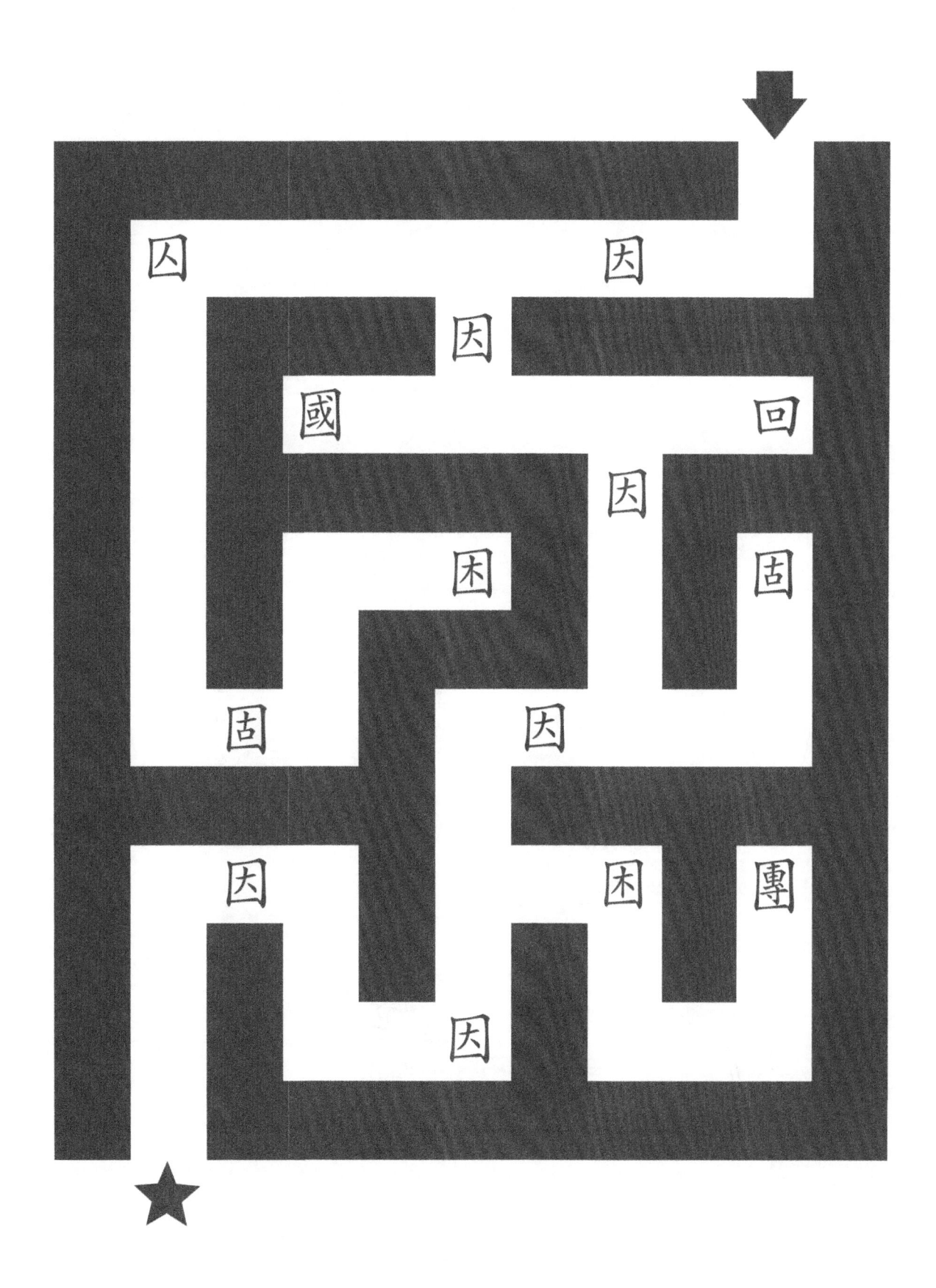

找到「因」字圈出來。
Find the characters 因 and circle them.

因　　　牛　　　因

　　　課　　　　

樂　　　　　首

　　　裡　　因

妹　　聲　　　

　　　音　　綠

唸唸看
Read-Aloud

- 妹妹因為上了音樂課，所以唱歌很好聽。
Because (my) little sister went to music class, therefore, she sings well.

- 他學會了六首歌。
She learned six songs.

- 他為什麼不唱《小白花》給我聽？
Why doesn't she sing Edelweiss for me?

- 因為他還沒學會。
Because she hasn't mastered it.

恭喜你完成了這一課，請回到第一頁將本課的愛心塗上顏色。
Congratulations! You have completed a lesson. Please color the heart for this lesson on page 1.

第十二課

Lesson 12 Zuò – to sit; to take (a bus, airplane etc.)

本書中的國字筆順是依據中華民國教育部「常用國字標準字體筆順學習網」的筆劃順序彙編。
The stroke orders of the characters in this workbook follow the stroke orders provided on the "Learning Program for Stroke Order of Frequently Used Chinese Characters" website of the Ministry of Education, R.O.C. (Taiwan).

請將文字連到對應的圖案。
Connect the characters to the correct pictures.

跑 •

坐 •

跳 •

47

請圈出與圖案相對應的句子。
Please circle the phrase that best describes the picture.

小狗很可愛。

我跑得很快。

坐在地上看書。

唸唸看
Read-Aloud

- 妹妹坐車去上中文課。
  (My) little sister goes to Chinese class by car.

- 我和小狗坐在外面等他。
  The little dog and I sit outside to wait for her.

- 我唱了一首歌給小狗聽。
  I sang a song for the little dog.

- 因為我很愛小狗。
  Because I love the little dog very much.

- 小狗也愛聽我唱歌。
  The little dog also loves to listen to me sing.

恭喜你完成了這一課,請回到第一頁將本課的愛心塗上顏色。
Congratulations! You have completed a lesson. Please color the heart for this lesson on page 1.

第十三課

Lesson 13 Shī – teacher; master; expert

本書中的國字筆順是依據中華民國教育部「常用國字標準字體筆順學習網」的筆劃順序彙編。
The stroke orders of the characters in this workbook follow the stroke orders provided on the "Learning Program for Stroke Order of Frequently Used Chinese Characters" website of the Ministry of Education, R.O.C. (Taiwan).

連連看
Connect the phrases to the correct pictures.

學生

老師

圖案中有的東西在（ ）中打勾。

Put a check next to the items that are in the picture.

（ ）書　　（ ）學生　（ ）狗
（ ）老師　（ ）花　　（ ）人
（ ）車　　（ ）樹　　（ ）同學

唸唸看
Read-Aloud

- 老師說上課時要坐好。
  The teacher says to sit still during class.

- 不可以跑跳。
  Do not run and jump.

- 我很快地把一首歌學會了。
  I quickly learned a song.

- 因為我有好好學，所以老師說我是好學生。
  Because I study hard, therefore, the teacher says I am a good student.

恭喜你完成了這一課，請回到第一頁將本課的愛心塗上顏色。
Congratulations! You have completed a lesson. Please color the heart for this lesson on page 1.

第十四課

Lesson 14 Jiāo – to teach
Jiào – religion teaching

本書中的國字筆順是依據中華民國教育部「常用國字標準字體筆順學習網」的筆劃順序彙編。
The stroke orders of the characters in this workbook follow the stroke orders provided on the "Learning Program for Stroke Order of Frequently Used Chinese Characters" website of the Ministry of Education, R.O.C. (Taiwan).

請跟著車子走並唸出路牌上的文字。
Read aloud the signs as the car drives through the road.

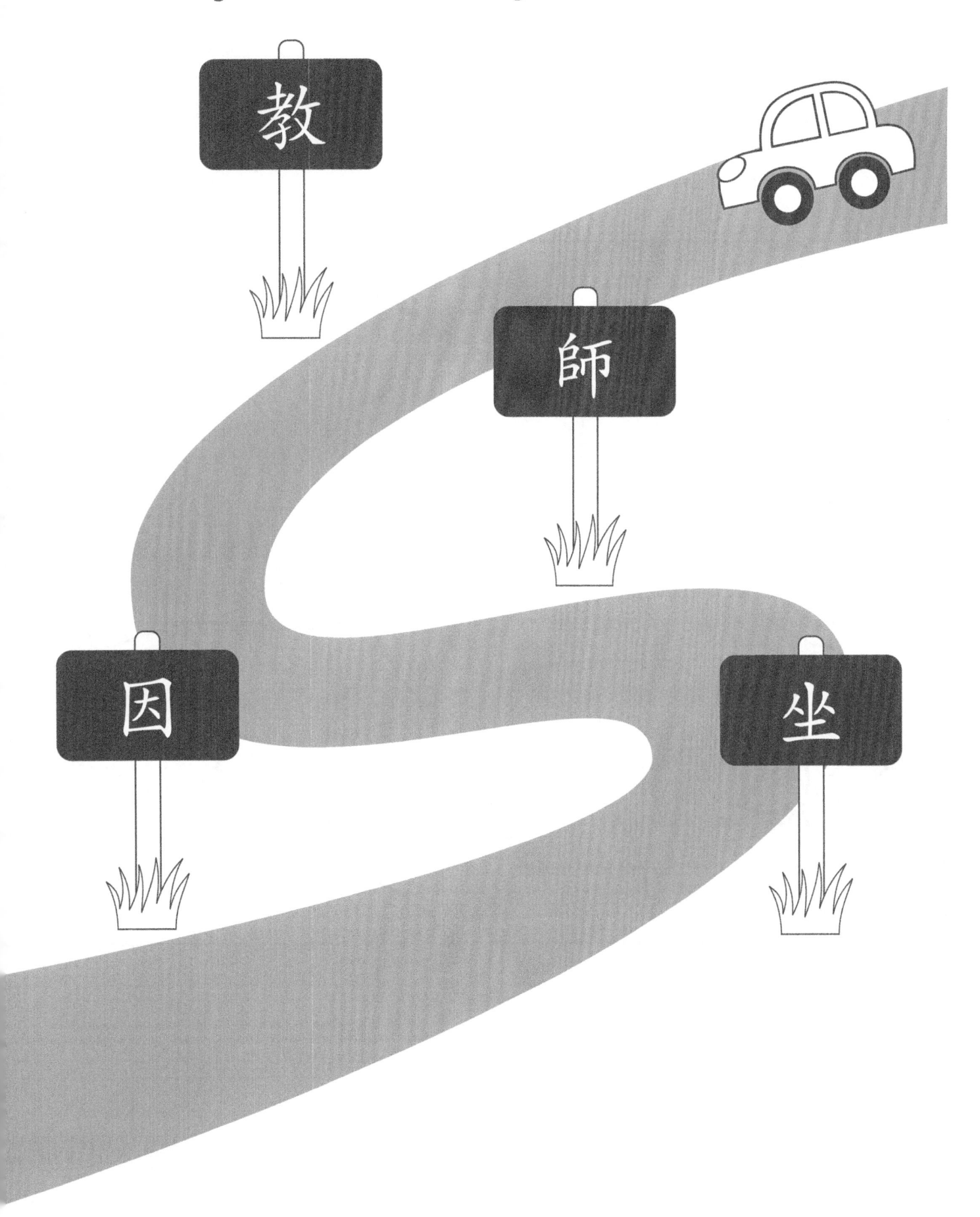

教

師

因

坐

請將有「教」字的地方著色。
Color the areas with the character 教.

唸唸看
Read-Aloud

- 老師教我們五首歌。
  The teacher taught us five songs.

- 因為老師教得很好，所以我們都學得很快。
  Because the teacher teaches well, therefore, we all learn fast.

- 我教小狗坐下。
  I teach the little dog to sit.

- 小狗也學得很快。
  The little dog also learns quickly.

- 所以我也是好老師。
  Therefore, I am also a good teacher.

恭喜你完成了這一課，請回到第一頁將本課的愛心塗上顏色。
Congratulations! You have completed a lesson. Please color the heart for this lesson on page 1.

第十五課

Lesson 15 Tóng – same; together

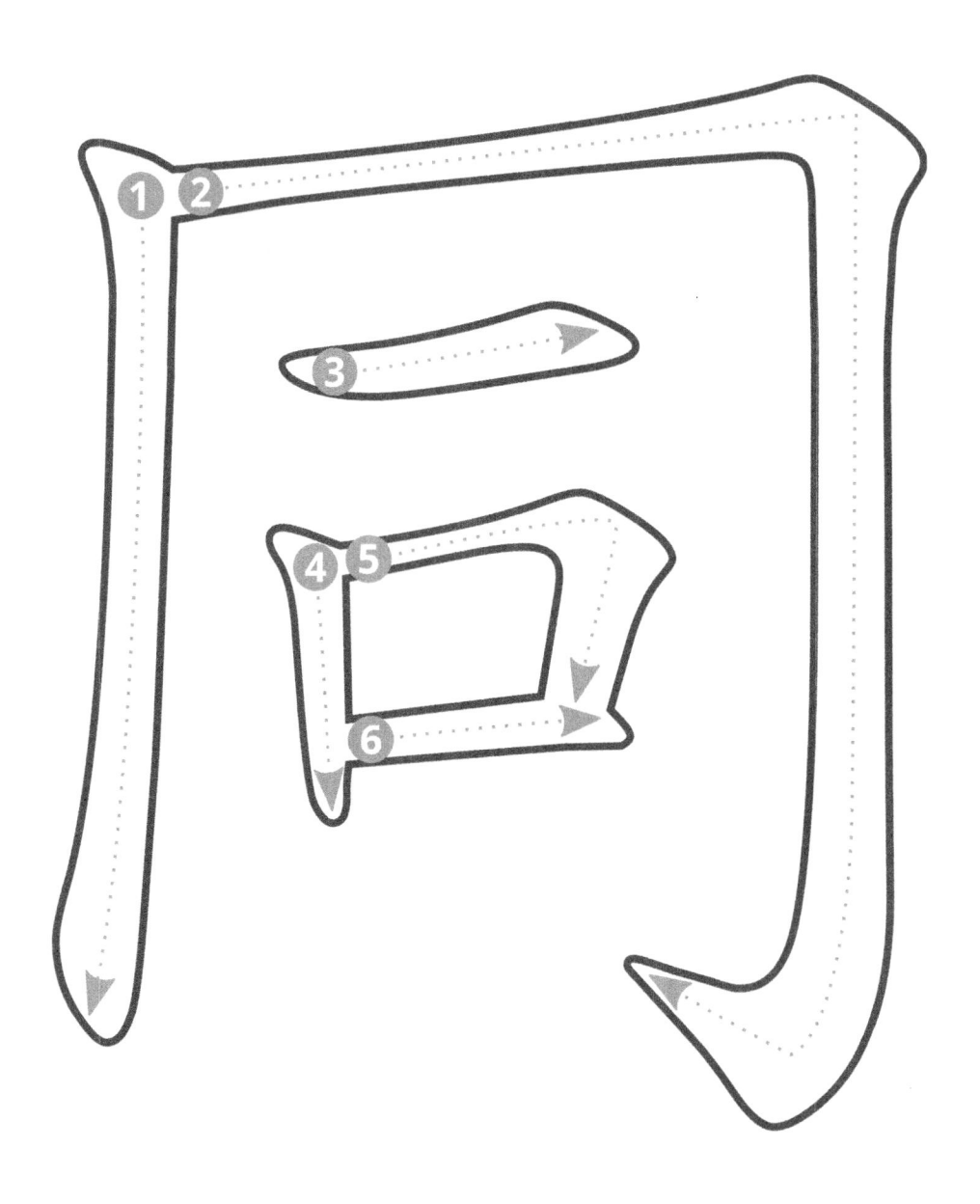

本書中的國字筆順是依據中華民國教育部「常用國字標準字體筆順學習網」的筆劃順序彙編。
The stroke orders of the characters in this workbook follow the stroke orders provided on the "Learning Program for Stroke Order of Frequently Used Chinese Characters" website of the Ministry of Education, R.O.C. (Taiwan).

在畫框內貼上或畫出你和一位同學的合影。
Paste or draw a picture of you and your classmate, and read aloud the characters at the bottom.

我和我的同學

請圈出兩隻完全相同的襪子。
Please circle the two identical socks.

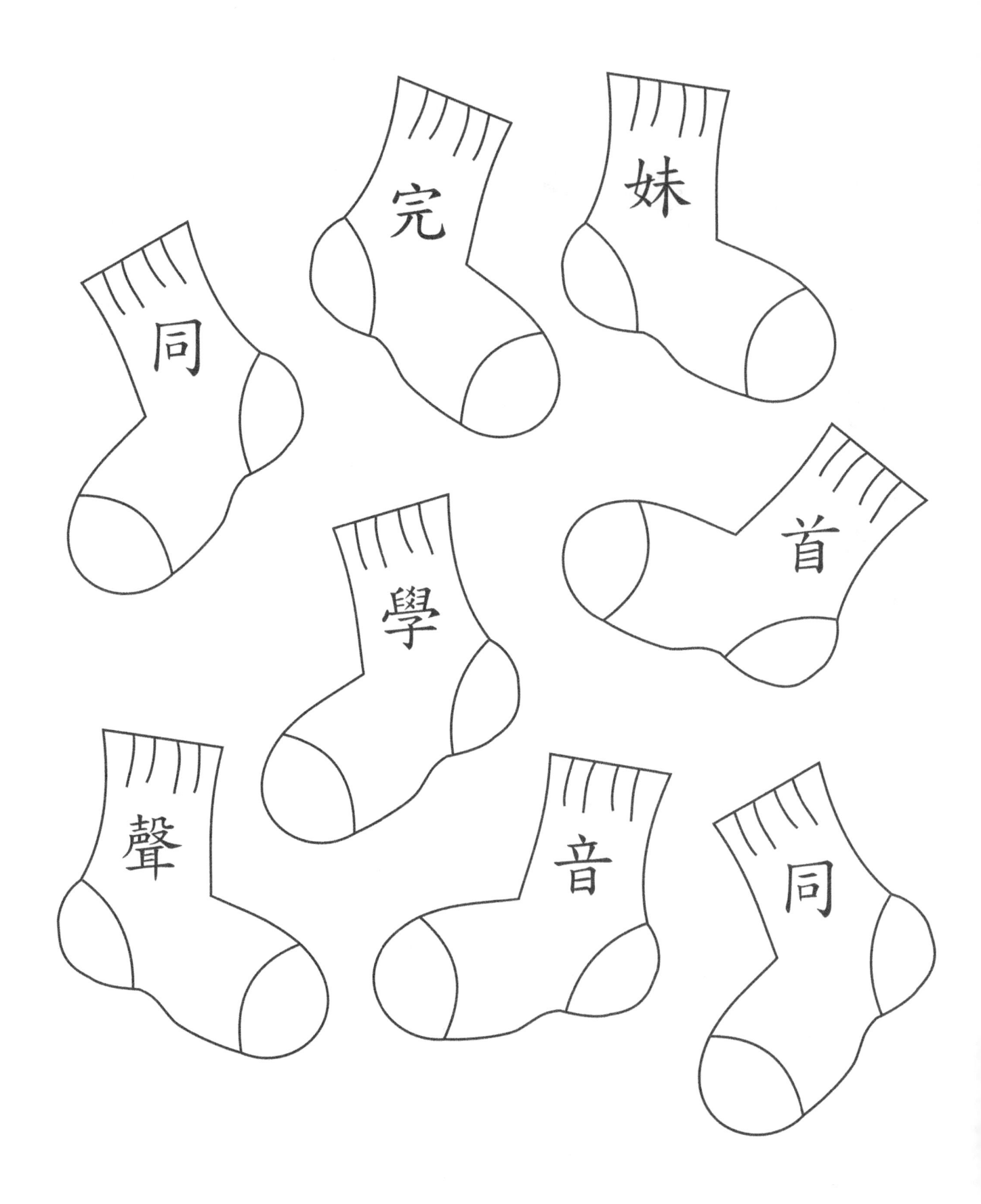

唸唸看
Read-Aloud

- 我有八個同學。
I have eight classmates.

- 我們坐著一起聽老師上課。
We sit together and listen to the teacher's lecture.

- 老師教我們太空人的故事。
The teacher teaches us a story about astronauts.

- 因為老師說得很生動，所以同學們都聽得很開心。
Because the teacher tells the story vividly, therefore, (my) classmates all enjoy listening.

恭喜你完成了這一課，請回到第一頁將本課的愛心塗上顏色。
Congratulations! You have completed a lesson. Please color the heart for this lesson on page 1.

62

第十六課

Lesson 16 Zì – character; word

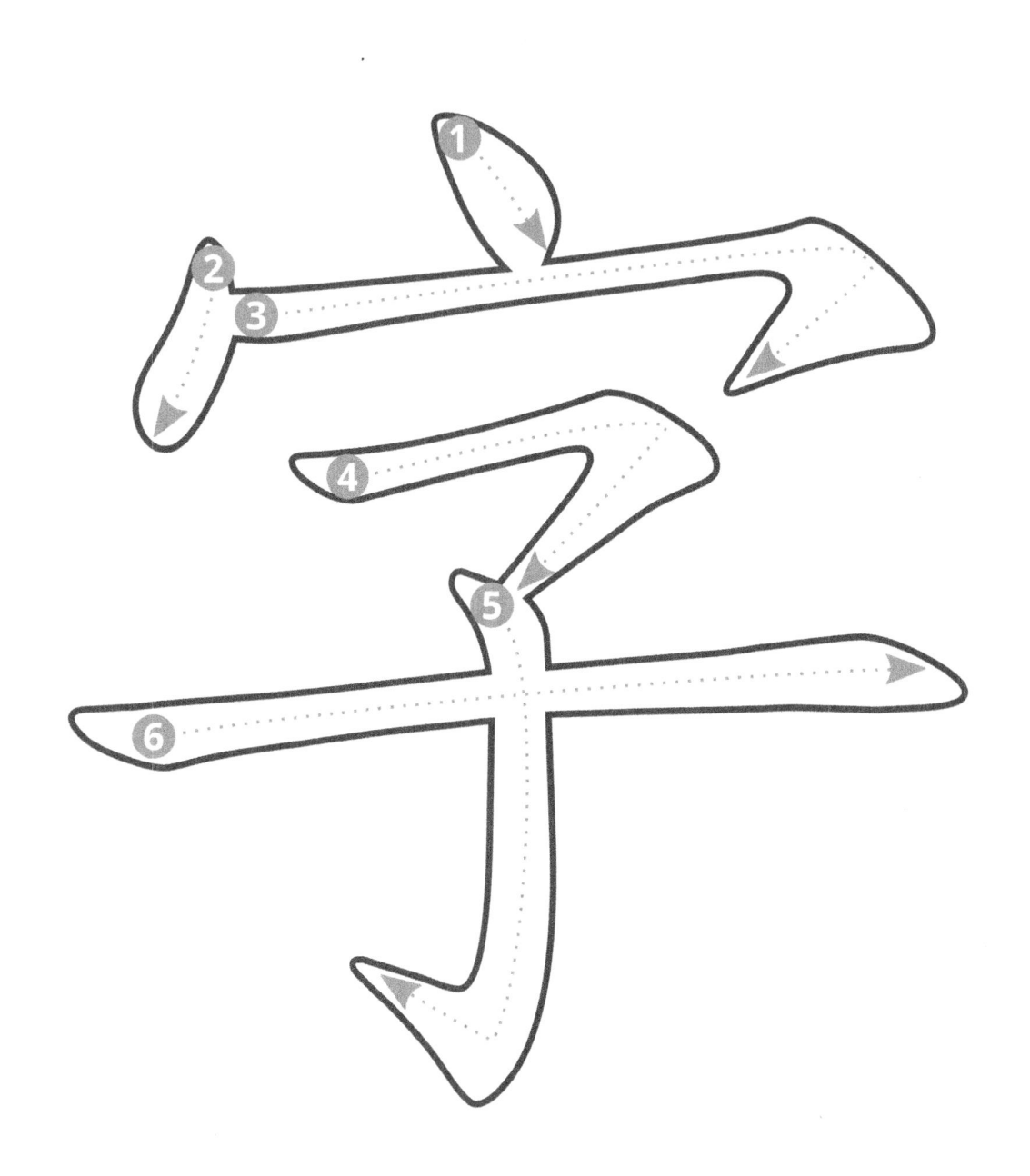

本書中的國字筆順是依據中華民國教育部「常用國字標準字體筆順學習網」的筆劃順序彙編。
The stroke orders of the characters in this workbook follow the stroke orders provided on the "Learning Program for Stroke Order of Frequently Used Chinese Characters" website of the Ministry of Education, R.O.C. (Taiwan).

請將「寫字」一詞連到寫字時會用到的物品上。
Connect the phrase 寫字 to the items used for writing.

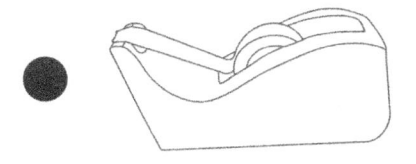

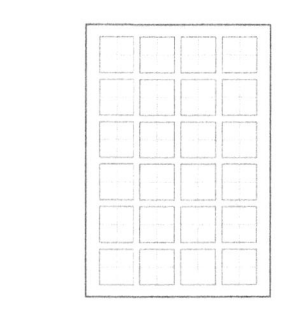

寫字

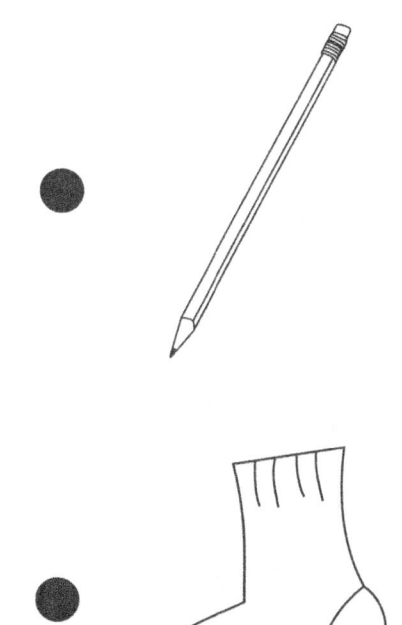

請將「寫字」一詞連到寫字時會用到的物品上。
Connect the phrase 寫字 to the items used for writing.

64

連連看一樣的字。
Draw a line to the matching character.

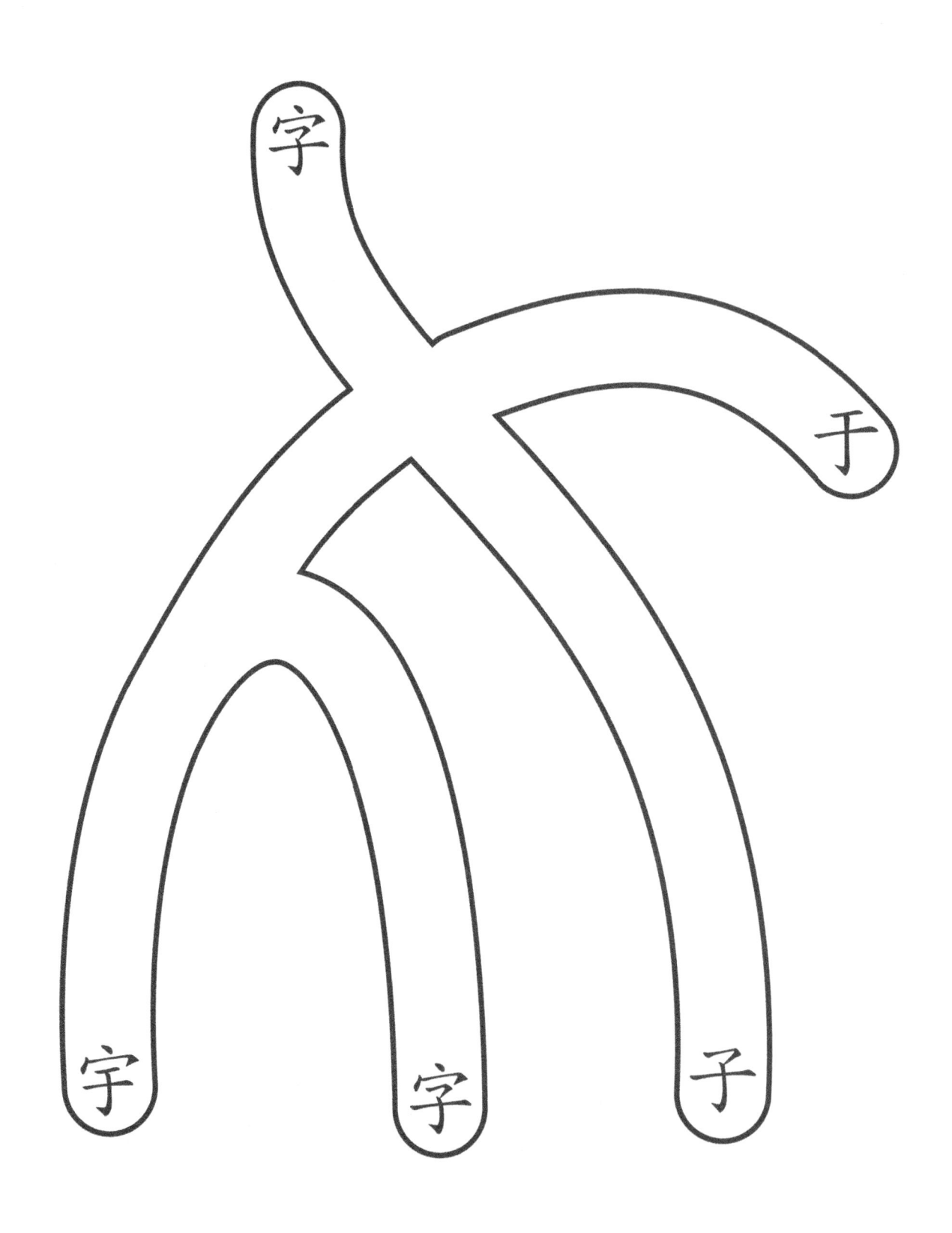

字 　 于

宇 　 字 　 子

唸唸看
Read-Aloud

- 老師教我們寫字前要先坐好。
The teacher teaches us to sit straight before writing.

- 同學們都很聽老師的話。
(My) classmates all listen to the teacher.

- 老師教了我們二十個生字。
The teacher taught us twenty new characters.

- 我們很用心學。
We learn diligently.

- 很快就能寫作了。
(We) will be able to compose essays soon.

恭喜你完成了這一課,請回到第一頁將本課的愛心塗上顏色。
Congratulations! You have completed a lesson. Please color the heart for this lesson on page 1.

第十七課

Lesson 17 Zhèng – positive; straight; upright; just; correct

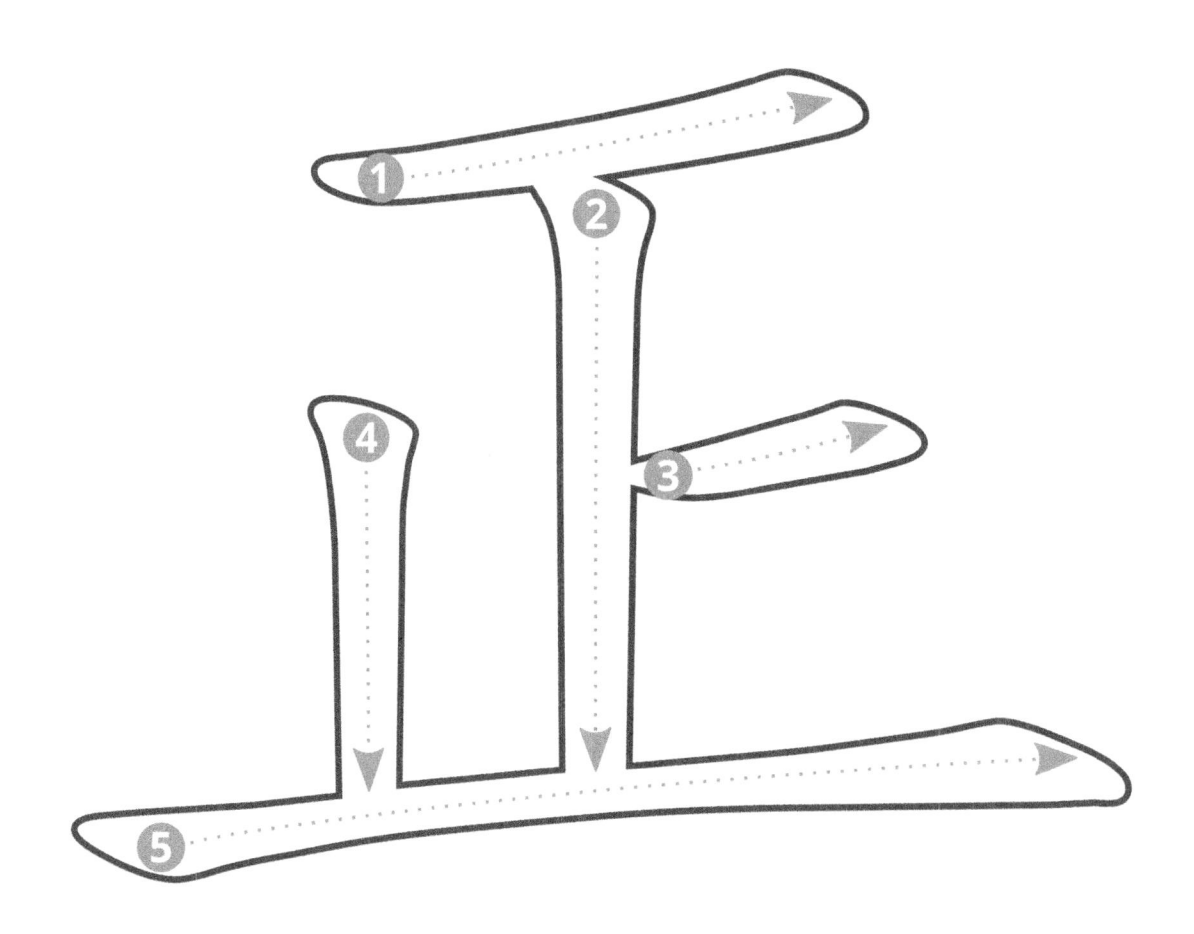

本書中的國字筆順是依據中華民國教育部「常用國字標準字體筆順學習網」的筆劃順序彙編。
The stroke orders of the characters in this workbook follow the stroke orders provided on the "Learning Program for Stroke Order of Frequently Used Chinese Characters" website of the Ministry of Education, R.O.C. (Taiwan).

找到「正」字圈出來。
Find the characters 正 and circle them.

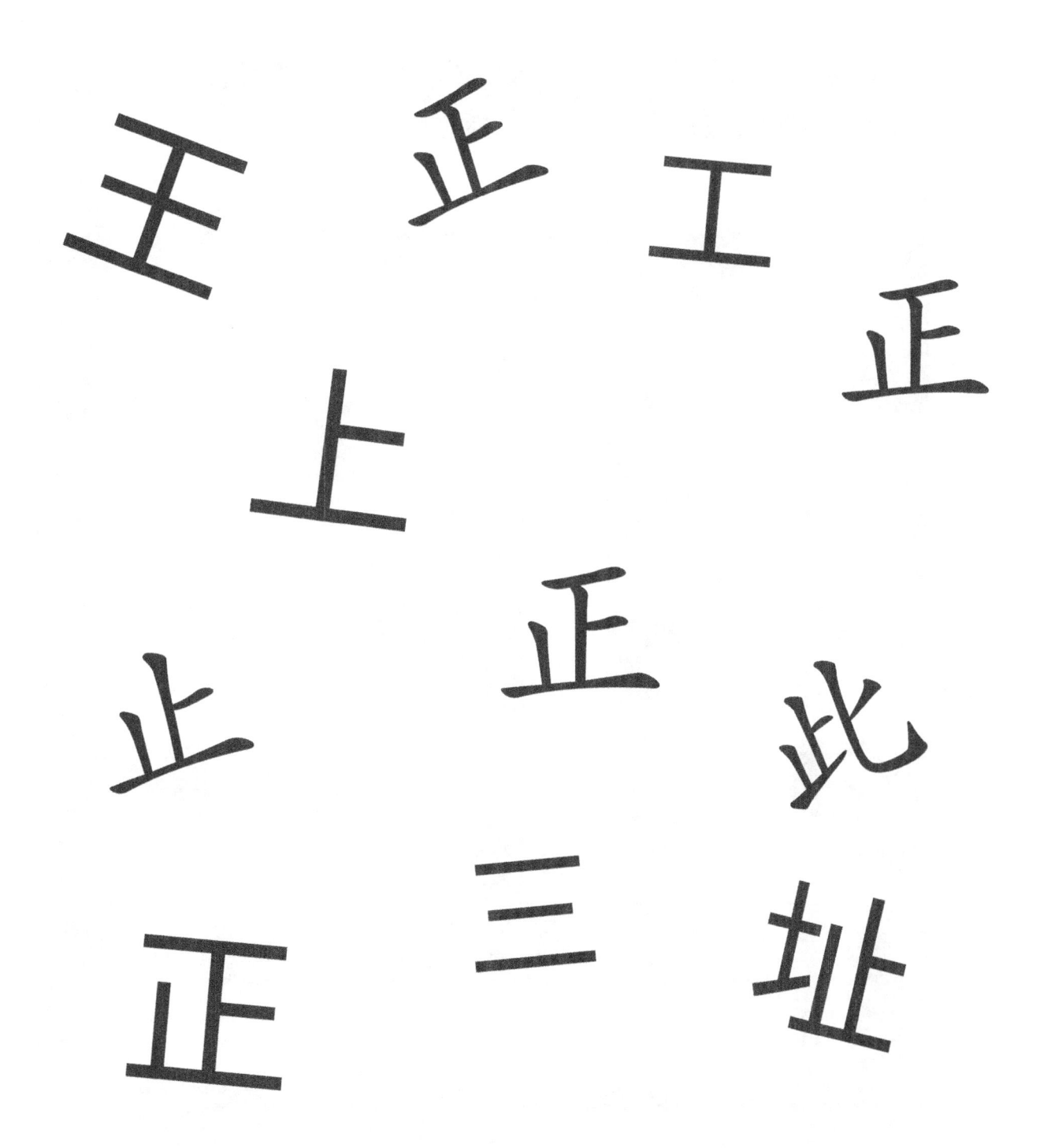

跟著「正」字從 ➡ 到 ★ 走出迷宮。
Follow the characters 正 from the arrow to the star to exit the maze.

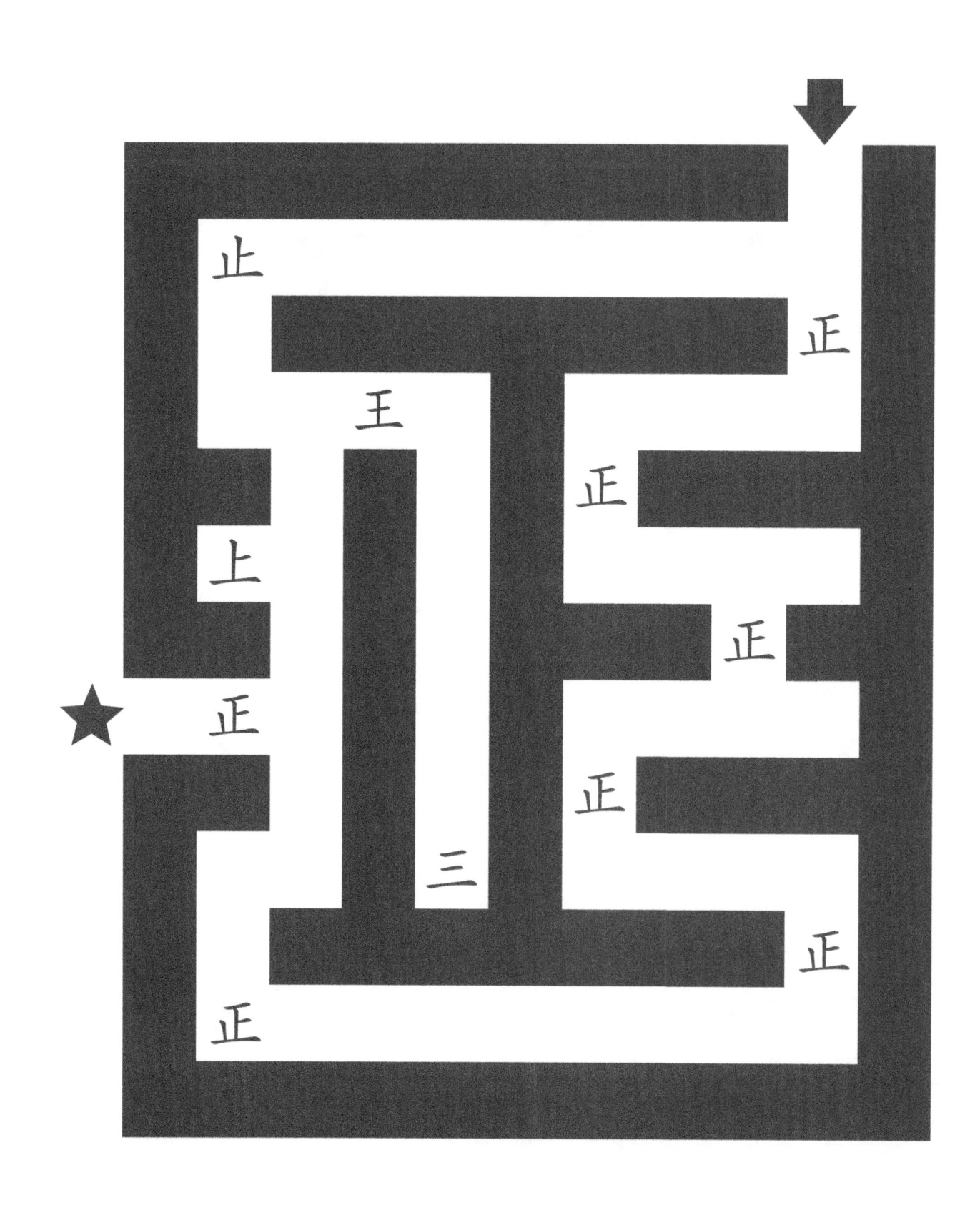

唸唸看
Read-Aloud

- 老師教同學寫字時，我看見外面有一隻兔子。

  When the teacher is teaching (my) classmate to write, I see a rabbit outside.

- 兔子正在吃紅色的花兒。

  The rabbit is eating red flowers.

- 兔子的耳朵很長，樣子也很可愛。

  The rabbit's ears are long, and (it) also looks very cute.

- 我正想要出去和兔子玩時，老師就叫我坐好。

  Just when I want to go out to play with the rabbit, the teacher tells me to sit down.

恭喜你完成了這一課，請回到第一頁將本課的愛心塗上顏色。
Congratulations! You have completed a lesson. Please color the heart for this lesson on page 1.

第十八課

Lesson 18 Měi – beautiful; good

本書中的國字筆順是依據中華民國教育部「常用國字標準字體筆順學習網」的筆劃順序彙編。
The stroke orders of the characters in this workbook follow the stroke orders provided on the "Learning Program for Stroke Order of Frequently Used Chinese Characters" website of the Ministry of Education, R.O.C. (Taiwan).

找到「美」字圈出來。
Find the characters 美 and circle them.

美　　　　正

　　　　　　同

　美　　　課

　　　　　　　字

　樂

　　　　　　　教

　　　　　坐

美

　　　　　綠　　　美

在字格中找出下列句子：

Find the following phrases in the grid:

1. 美好的日子
2. 美美的天空
3. 美國很大

美	好	的	日	子
美	國	很	大	首
的	樂	聲	正	家
天	教	音	等	坐
空	綠	妹	師	牛

唸唸看
Read-Aloud

- 老師教同學寫字時，我也用心看。

   When the teacher is teaching (my) classmate to write, I watch diligently as well.

- 老師寫的字很美。

   The teacher's writing is beautiful.

- 我也想要寫出那麼美的字。

   I also want to write beautiful characters.

- 我正要動手寫字時，就下課了。

   Just when I start to write, the class is dismissed.

- 只好明日再寫了。

   So I can only write tomorrow.

恭喜你完成了這一課，請回到第一頁將本課的愛心塗上顏色。
Congratulations! You have completed a lesson. Please color the heart for this lesson on page 1.

第十九課

Lesson 19 Lì – beautiful

本書中的國字筆順是依據中華民國教育部「常用國字標準字體筆順學習網」的筆劃順序彙編。
The stroke orders of the characters in this workbook follow the stroke orders provided on the "Learning Program for Stroke Order of Frequently Used Chinese Characters" website of the Ministry of Education, R.O.C. (Taiwan).

請跟著帆船行駛念出牌子上的文字。
Read aloud the signs as the boat sails down the river.

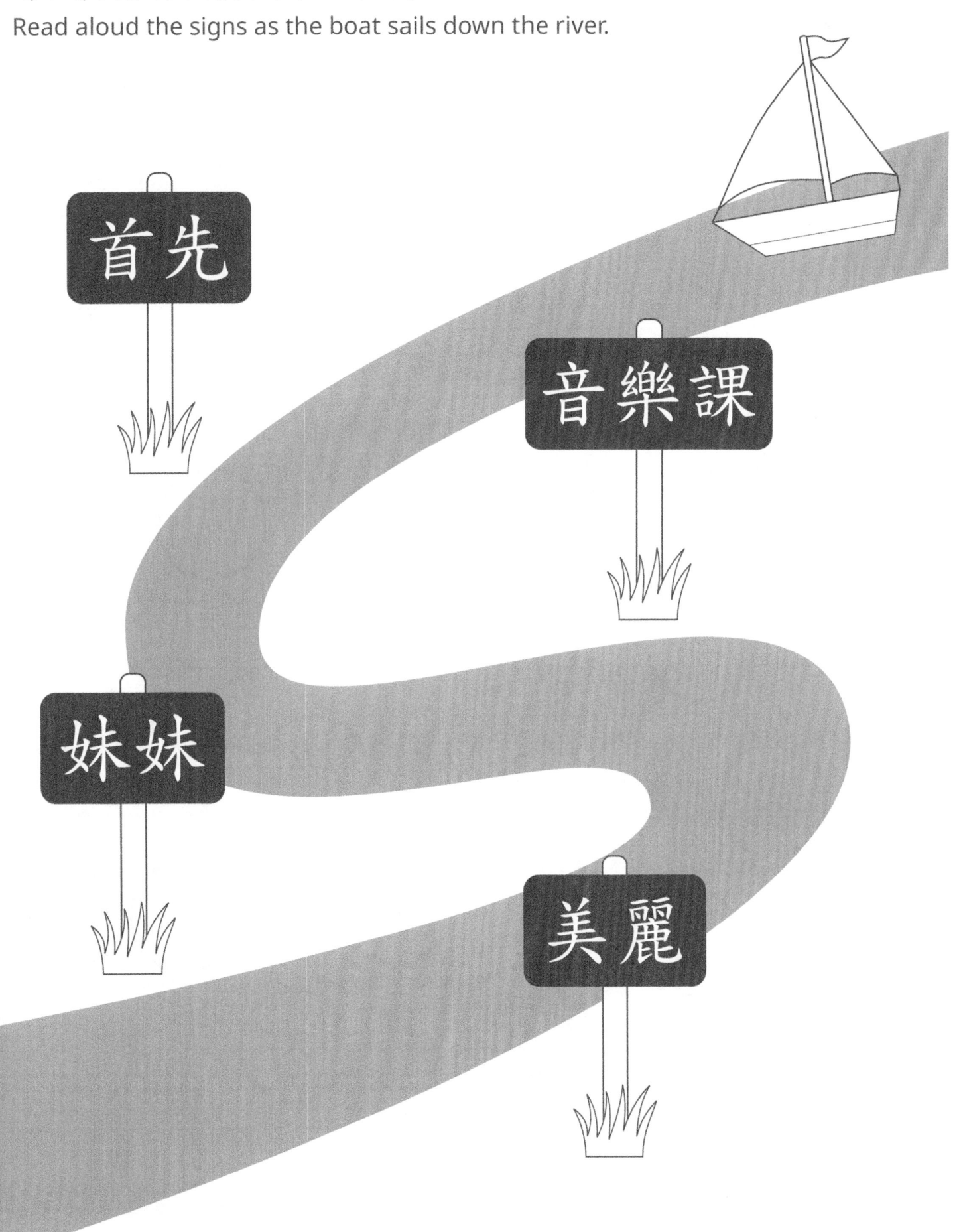

- 首先
- 音樂課
- 妹妹
- 美麗

76

將「麗」字塗色幫兩隻小狗會面。
Color the characters 麗 to guide the dogs together.

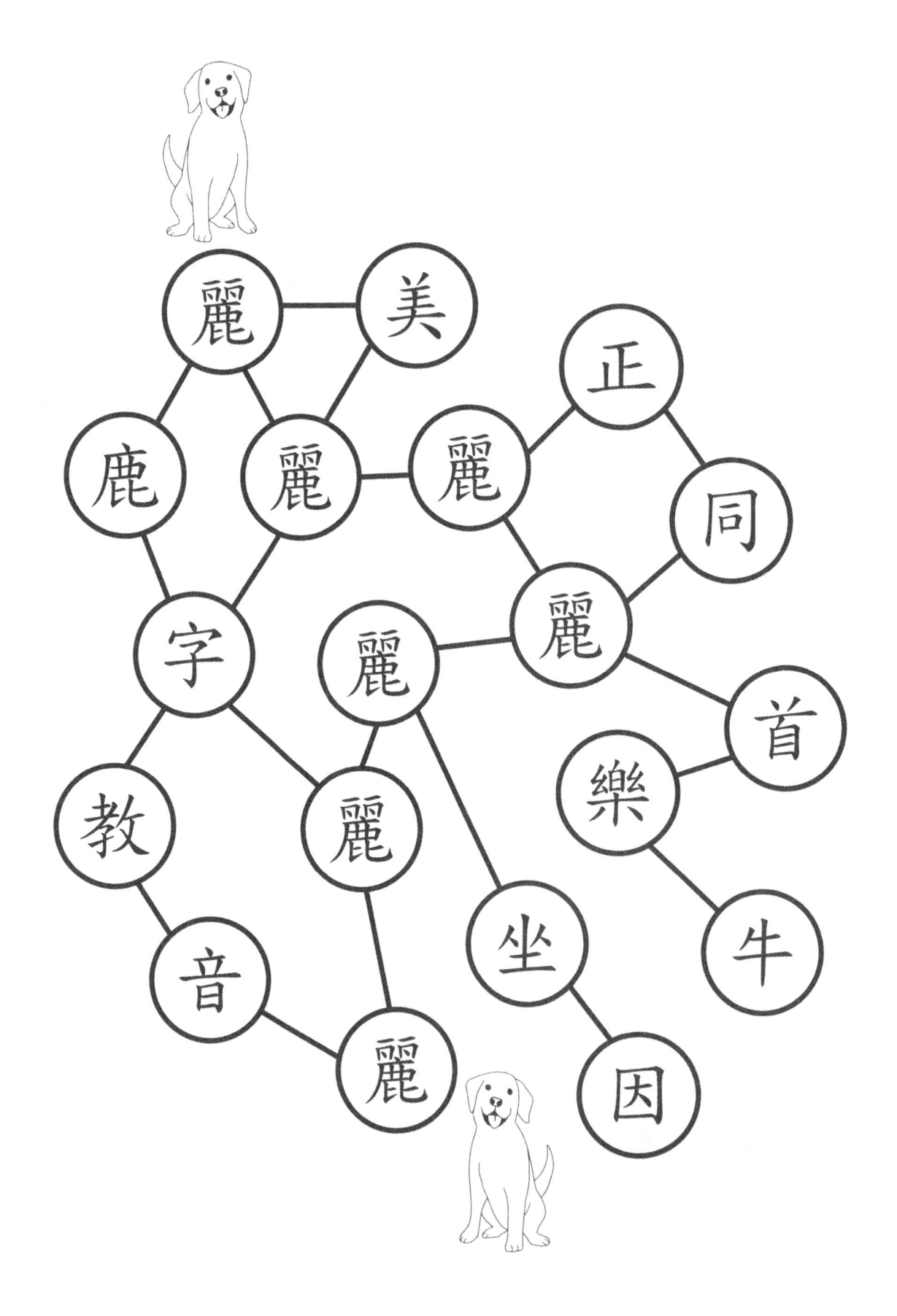

唸唸看
Read-Aloud

- 媽媽正在說故事給我聽。
  Mom is telling me a story.

- 我的媽媽長得很美麗。
  My mom is very beautiful.

- 還會教我寫中文字。
  (She) also teaches me how to write Chinese characters.

- 媽媽寫的字也很美麗。
  Mom's writing is also beautiful.

- 我想和媽媽一同出去玩。
  I want to go out to play with Mom.

恭喜你完成了這一課,請回到第一頁將本課的愛心塗上顏色。
Congratulations! You have completed a lesson. Please color the heart for this lesson on page 1.

第二十課

Lesson 20 Fāng – square; place; direction; method

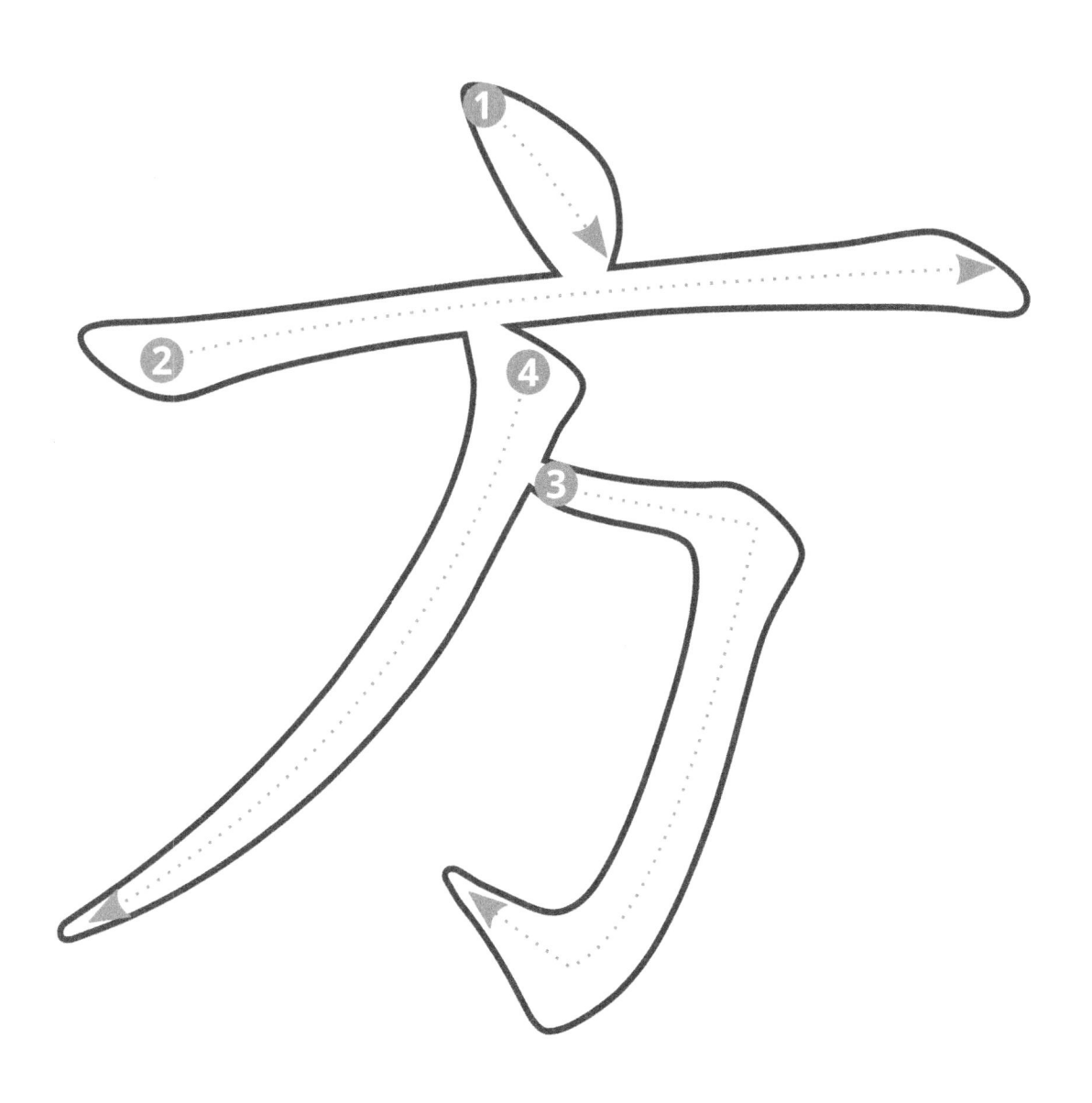

本書中的國字筆順是依據中華民國教育部「常用國字標準字體筆順學習網」的筆劃順序彙編。
The stroke orders of the characters in this workbook follow the stroke orders provided on the "Learning Program for Stroke Order of Frequently Used Chinese Characters" website of the Ministry of Education, R.O.C. (Taiwan).

找到「方」字圈出來。
Find the characters 方 and circle them.

教　　　　　弟

同

　　　方

　　　　　師

　　　方

美　　　　　正

　　文　　　字

麗　　　　方

80

請將三個相同的物品連成一線。
Please connect the same items to win the tic-tac-toe.

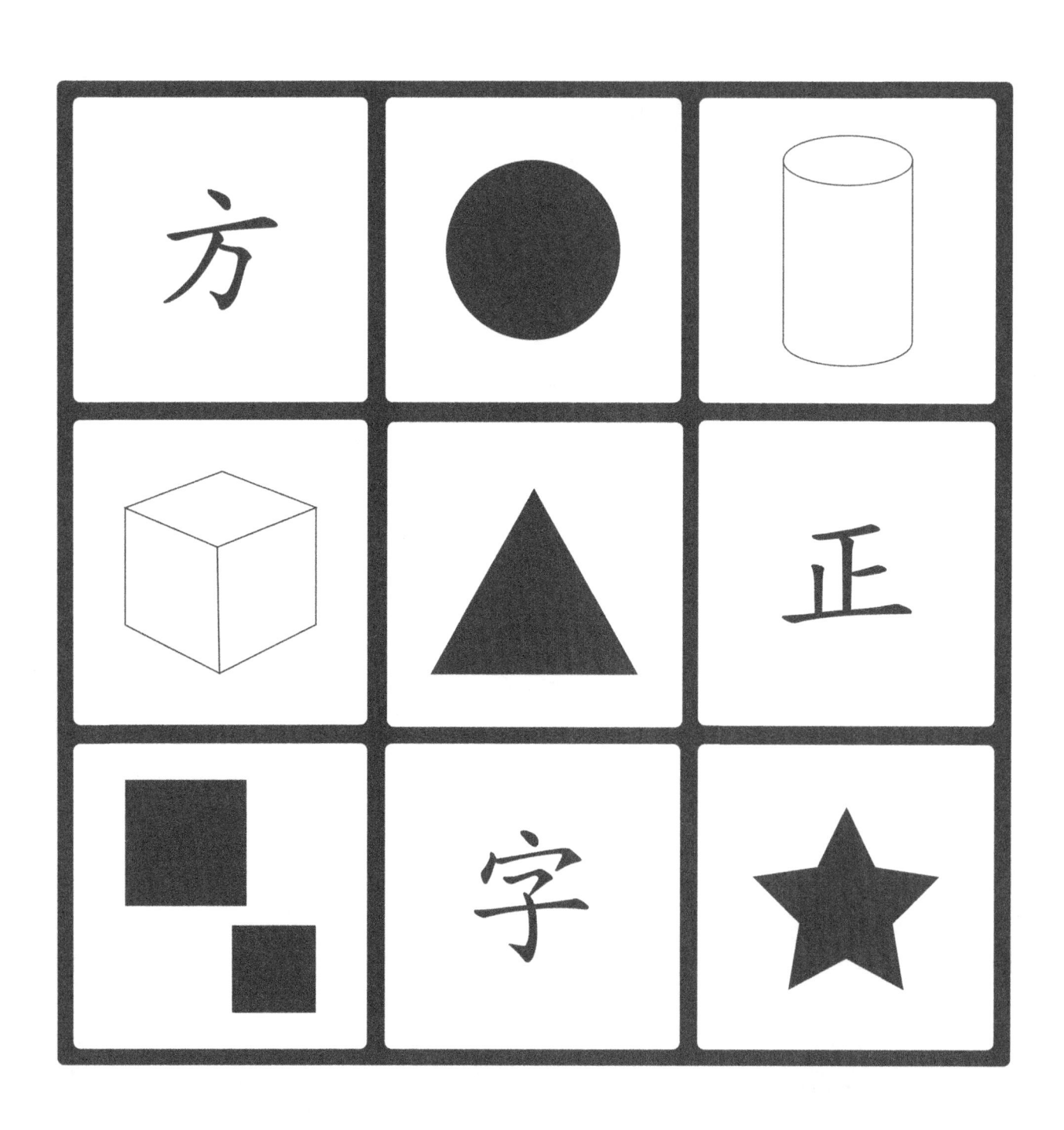

唸唸看
Read-Aloud

- 妹妹寫的字很方正。
  (My) little sister writes neatly.

- 老師說這樣很美麗。
  The teacher says this is beautiful.

- 我和妹妹一起寫故事。
  (My) little sister and I write stories together.

- 我的字也很方正。
  My writing also is very neat.

- 我們寫的字看起來一樣。
  Our writing looks the same.

恭喜你完成了這一課,請回到第一頁將本課的愛心塗上顏色。
Congratulations! You have completed a lesson. Please color the heart for this lesson on page 1.

82

第二十一課

Lesson 21 Guó – country; nation

本書中的國字筆順是依據中華民國教育部「常用國字標準字體筆順學習網」的筆劃順序彙編。
The stroke orders of the characters in this workbook follow the stroke orders provided on the "Learning Program for Stroke Order of Frequently Used Chinese Characters" website of the Ministry of Education, R.O.C. (Taiwan).

請畫出你的國旗並唸出下方的文字。
Please draw your national flag and read aloud the characters below.

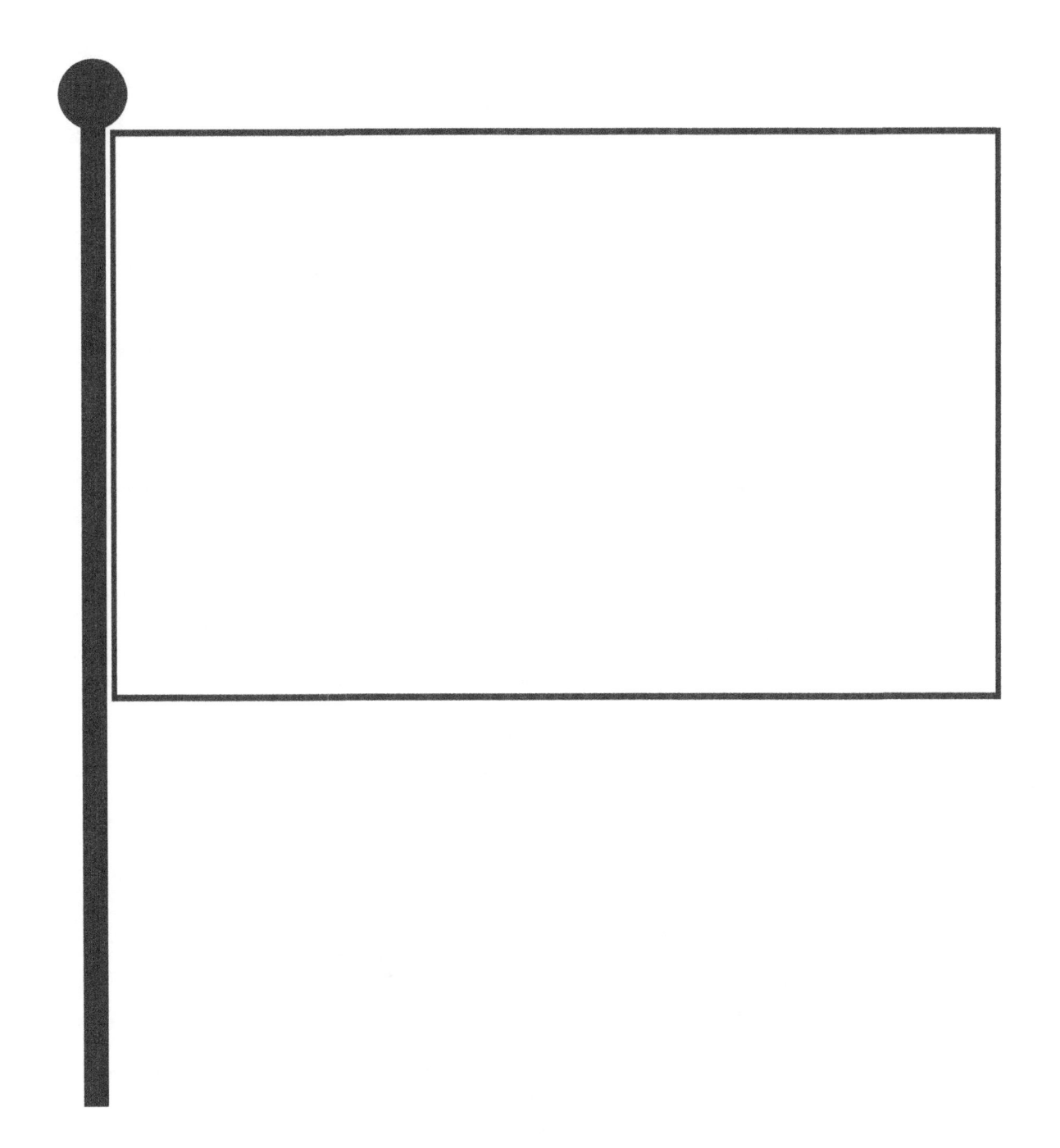

我愛我的國家

在字格中找出下列句子：

Find the following phrases in the grid:

1. 美麗的國家

2. 好聽的音樂

因	等	好	同	字
完	牛	聽	妹	課
美	麗	的	國	家
方	聲	音	教	坐
正	綠	樂	師	首

唸唸看
Read-Aloud

- 你的國家是一個很美麗的地方。
  Your country is a beautiful place.

- 那裡有藍藍的天空和很大的土地。
  There are blue sky and vast land there.

- 我正想要出國去玩。
  I am thinking to travel abroad.

- 我們一同去你的國家玩,好不好?
  Let's visit your country together, okay?

恭喜你完成了這一課,請回到第一頁將本課的愛心塗上顏色。
Congratulations! You have completed a lesson. Please color the heart for this lesson on page 1.

第二十二課

Lesson 22 Yuè – moon; month

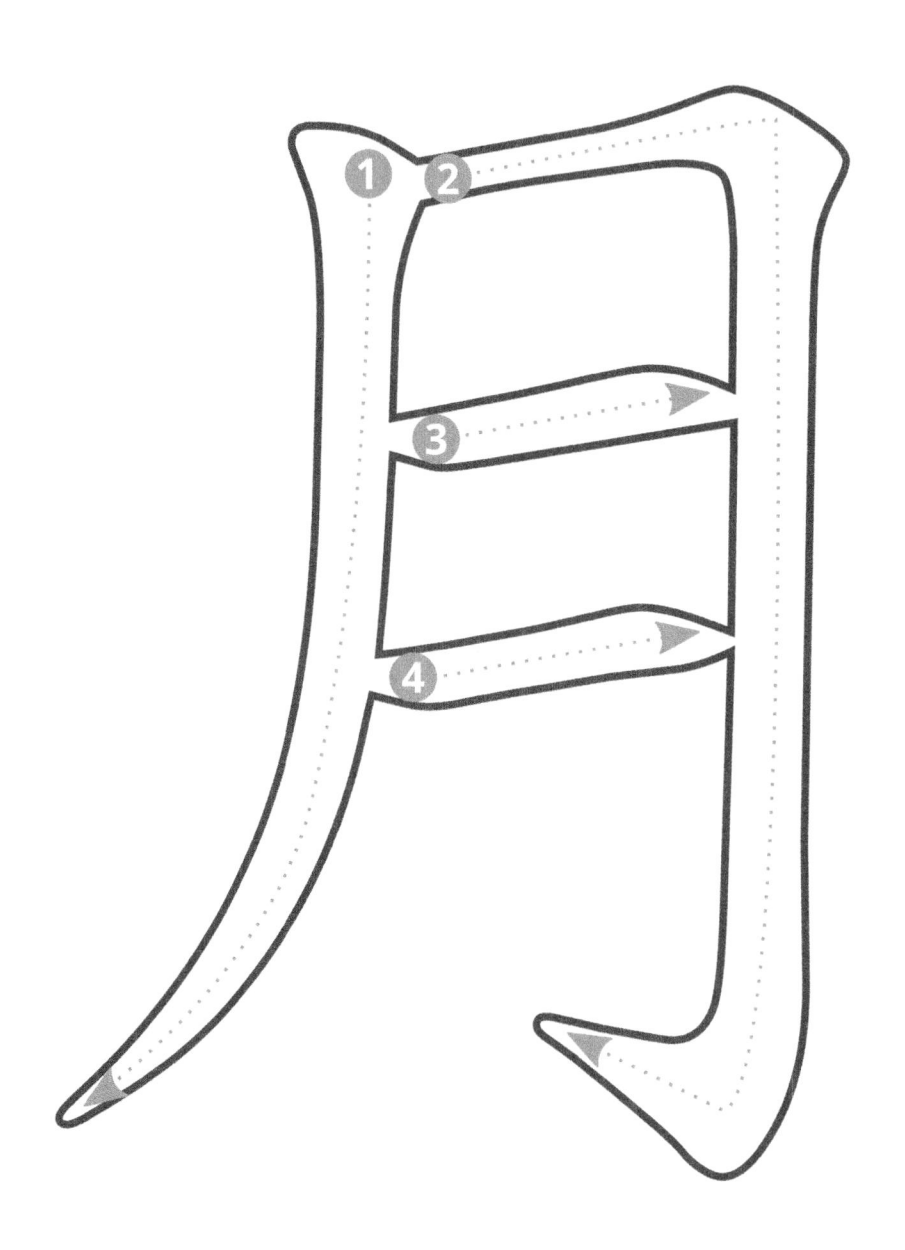

本書中的國字筆順是依據中華民國教育部「常用國字標準字體筆順學習網」的筆劃順序彙編。
The stroke orders of the characters in this workbook follow the stroke orders provided on the "Learning Program for Stroke Order of Frequently Used Chinese Characters" website of the Ministry of Education, R.O.C. (Taiwan).

「月」是象形字，它是彎月的樣子演變來的。
The character 月 is a pictograph. It looks like a crescent moon.

連連看
Connect the characters to the correct items in the picture.

日　　月　　山　　雲

唸唸看
Read-Aloud

- 這個月我們要去美國玩。
  We are going to visit the U.S.A. this month.

- 下個月我們要去中國玩。
  We are going to visit China next month.

- 我們會去好多地方。
  We will go to many places.

- 兩個國家都好美麗。
  Both countries are beautiful.

恭喜你完成了這一課,請回到第一頁將本課的愛心塗上顏色。
Congratulations! You have completed a lesson. Please color the heart for this lesson on page 1.

第二十三課

Lesson 23 Jiǔ – nine

本書中的國字筆順是依據中華民國教育部「常用國字標準字體筆順學習網」的筆劃順序彙編。
The stroke orders of the characters in this workbook follow the stroke orders provided on the "Learning Program for Stroke Order of Frequently Used Chinese Characters" website of the Ministry of Education, R.O.C. (Taiwan).

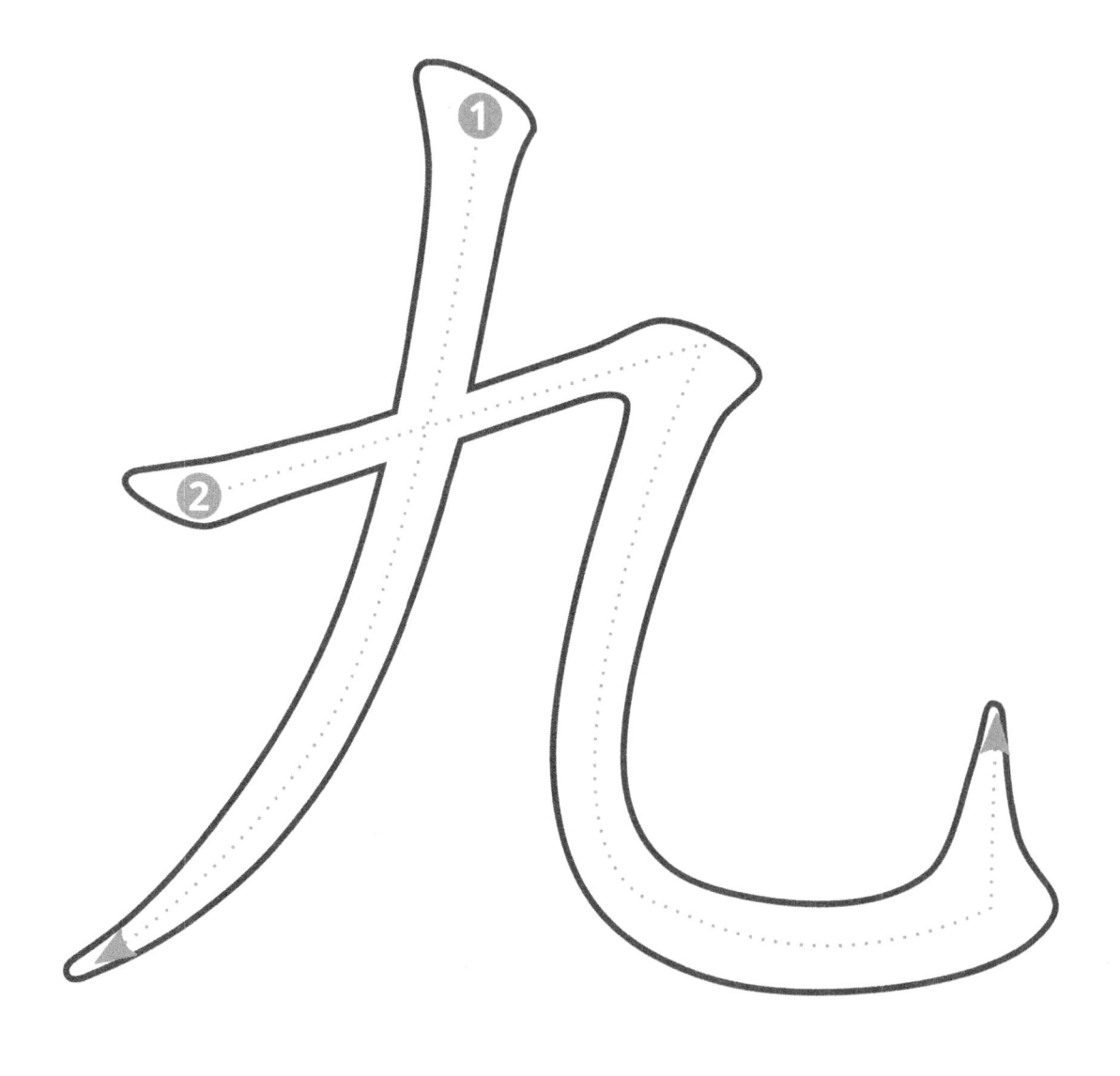

連連看
Connect the dots to complete the picture.

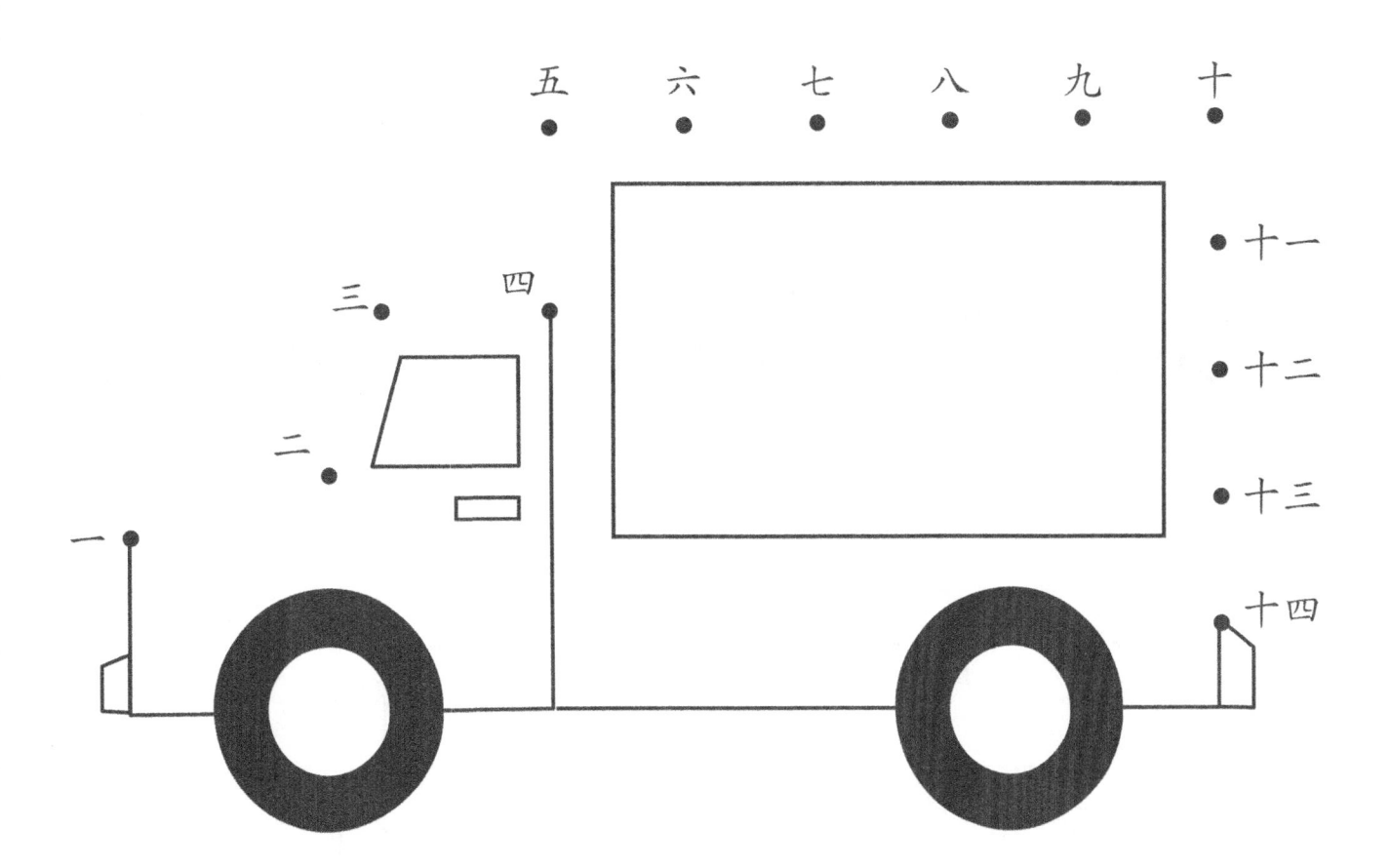

91

92

請觀察列車上數字的順序並剪下下方的字格貼到正確的車箱中。
Please observe the pattern, cut out the characters at the bottom, and paste them into the correct cargo.

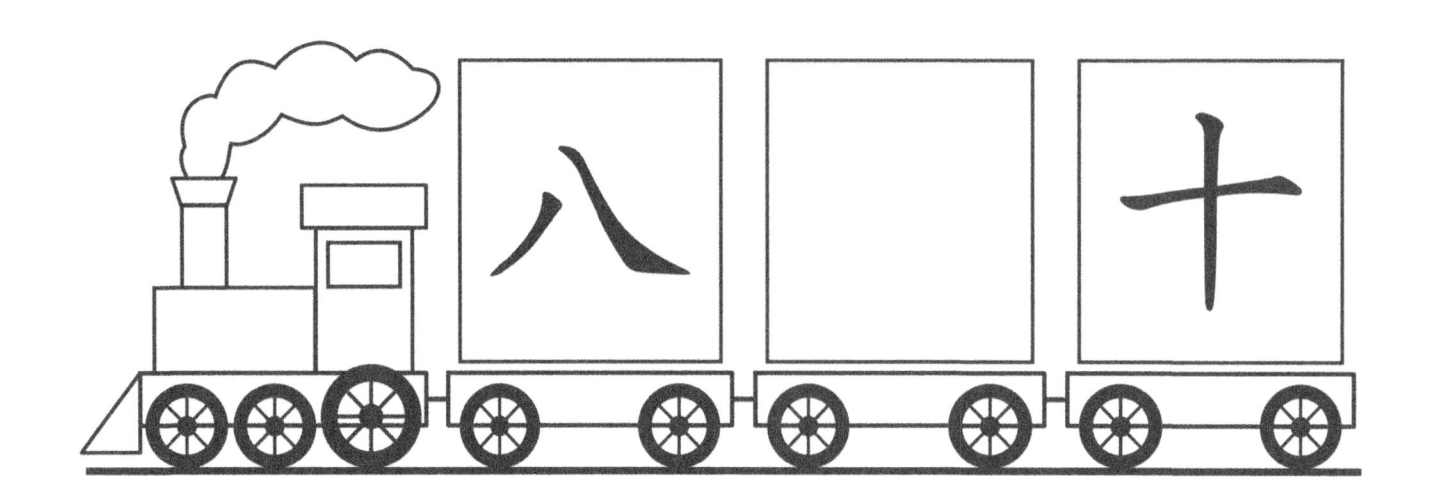

五 六 九 九 十

唸唸看
Read-Aloud

- 九月時我們會出國去玩。
In September, we will travel abroad.

- 我們會去九個國家。
We will visit nine countries.

- 有的地方很美麗，有的很好玩。
Some places are beautiful, some are fun.

- 因為我們很開心要出國玩，所以我和弟弟一起快樂地唱了好幾首歌。
Because we are excited to travel abroad, therefore, (my) little brother and I happily sing many songs together.

恭喜你完成了這一課，請回到第一頁將本課的愛心塗上顏色。
Congratulations! You have completed a lesson. Please color the heart for this lesson on page 1.

第二十四課

Lesson 24 Rán – correct; right; so; thus; however

本書中的國字筆順是依據中華民國教育部「常用國字標準字體筆順學習網」的筆劃順序彙編。
The stroke orders of the characters in this workbook follow the stroke orders provided on the "Learning Program for Stroke Order of Frequently Used Chinese Characters" website of the Ministry of Education, R.O.C. (Taiwan).

95

將「然」字塗色，幫松鼠找到回家的路。
Color the characters 然 to find the path home.

		音			
綠	麗	自		然	
九		然	然	然	師
美		然			樂
月		然	燃	聲	教
國		然			首

96

請將下方的圖案剪下來，分別貼到對應的位置。
Paste the items to the corresponding categories.

天然　｜　不是天然

唸唸看
Read-Aloud

- 九月我們要去美國玩。
In September, we are visiting the U.S.A.

- 我們會先去美國然後再去中國。
We will first go to the U.S.A. then go to China.

- 我們會先開車然後再走路上山。
We will first drive then hike up the mountain.

- 我們會去好多地方。
We will go to many places.

恭喜你完成了這一課,請回到第一頁將本課的愛心塗上顏色。
Congratulations! You have completed a lesson. Please color the heart for this lesson on page 1.

第二十五課

Lesson 25 Zì – self; oneself; from; since

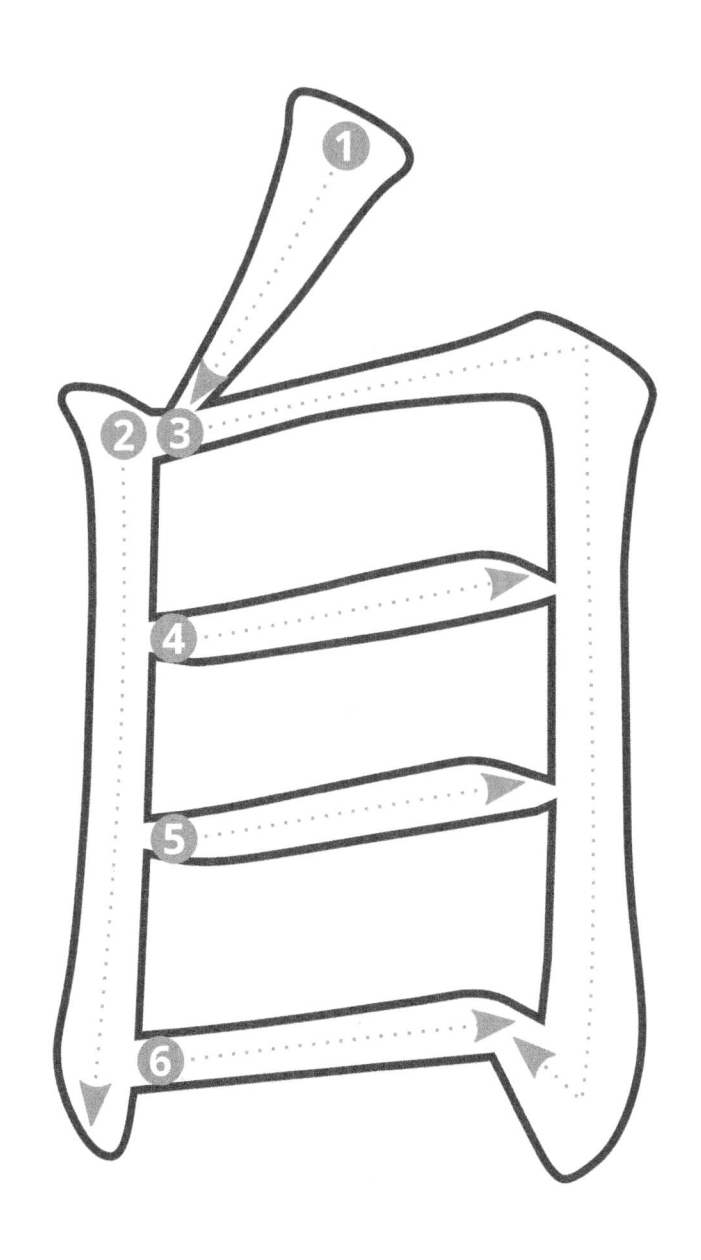

本書中的國字筆順是依據中華民國教育部「常用國字標準字體筆順學習網」的筆劃順序彙編。
The stroke orders of the characters in this workbook follow the stroke orders provided on the "Learning Program for Stroke Order of Frequently Used Chinese Characters" website of the Ministry of Education, R.O.C. (Taiwan).

跟著「自」字從 ➡ 到 ★ 走出迷宮。
Follow the characters 自 from the arrow to the star to exit the maze.

請跟著女孩走並唸出路牌上的文字。
Read aloud the signs as the girl walks down the path.

自然

九月

美麗

聲音

唸唸看
Read-Aloud

- 美國有很多大自然的地方。
There are many natural places in the U.S.A.

- 大自然裡有很多綠綠的樹。
There are many green trees in nature.

- 大自然裡的空氣也很好。
The air is also fresh in nature.

- 我很開心九月就要到那裡玩了。
I am very happy to visit there in September.

恭喜你完成了這一課，請回到第一頁將本課的愛心塗上顏色。
Congratulations! You have completed a lesson. Please color the heart for this lesson on page 1.

獎狀
Certificate of Achievement

恭喜

Congratulations to

_____

完成趣味識字第七冊。
特發此狀以資鼓勵！

for completing Fun with Chinese Workbook 7.

_____ _____

簽名 Signature 日期 Date

Made in the USA
Las Vegas, NV
01 May 2025